D0144074

John McCormick is Professor of European Union Politics at Indiana University, USA. He originally trained in journalism and worked for eight years in the information departments of two London-based environmental interest groups before becoming an academic, since when he has published a wide range of books on the EU and other subjects including Understanding European Integration *(now in its 5th edition),* The European Union, The European Superpower *and* Contemporary Britain.

Visit John McCormick's website at http://johnmccormick.eu for the latest commentary on Europe and the EU.

'McCormick's clear, concrete exposition of the importance of the EU to all its Member States and citizens will inform and enlighten Euro enthusiasts and sceptics alike – could not have been more timely for the new debate about Britain's role in a changing Union' – John Palmer, formerly European editor of the *Guardian* and founder political director of the European Policy Centre.

'A must read for citizens, professionals, students and policy-makers alike by one of the most respected authorities on European Affairs.' – Alexander Stubb, Minister for European Affairs and Foreign Trade, Finland

'Sceptical voices have been a constant accompaniment to the construction of a Europe "united in diversity" and, as John McCormick reminds us, there have been many memorable predictions over the years of its impending crisis or death. With his wide knowledge of history and expertise as a seasoned political analyst, he is well aware of both the strengths and weaknesses of this process and of the inevitability of periods of stagnation and crisis as well as periods of dynamism. But in a stark challenge to sceptics and critics he shows that the story of European Union has been, above all, one of progress in mutual understanding between peoples, of the benefits of cooperation and of the pooling of sovereignty between nations, and of a growing solidarity and cohesion in practice that could provide a model too for those looking for a more peaceful and cooperative form of organization on a global scale.' – Jacques Delors, former president of the European Commission

Why Europe Matters

The Case for the European Union

John McCormick

First published 2013 by
PALGRAVE MACMILLAN

Palgrave Macmillan in the UK is an imprint of Macmillan Publishers Limited, registered in England, company number 785998, of Houndmills, Basingstoke, Hampshire RG21 6XS.

Palgrave Macmillan in the US is a division of St Martin's Press LLC, 175 Fifth Avenue, New York, NY 10010.

Palgrave Macmillan is the global academic imprint of the above companies and has companies and representatives throughout the world.

Palgrave® and Macmillan® are registered trademarks in the United States, the United Kingdom, Europe and other countries

ISBN: 978–1–137–01688–1 hardback
ISBN: 978–1–137–01687–4 paperback

This book is printed on paper suitable for recycling and made from fully managed and sustained forest sources. Logging, pulping and manufacturing processes are expected to conform to the environmental regulations of the country of origin.

A catalogue record for this book is available from the British Library.

A catalog record for this book is available from the Library of Congress.

Contents

List of Illustrations

Figures

Tables

Boxes

Document

Map

Preface and Acknowledgements

Europe has been dominating the headlines of late, but rarely for happy reasons. First we had the breaking in 2009 of the sovereign debt crisis in Greece, and it was not long before the woes of one small European country took on deeper and wider significance: worries about contagion grew, euro zone leaders were divided over how to respond, there was talk of exits from the euro, the very viability of the single currency was questioned, and there were doubts even about the future of the European Union. It became hard to find anyone prepared to step up in praise of integration, and even long-standing pro-Europeans struggled to maintain their sunny dispositions.

As the euro zone crisis deepened in late 2011, I was asked to write a chapter making the case for the EU in a university textbook.[1] The exercise made me realize that while more than 20 years of studying and writing about the EU had left me convinced of the benefits and advantages of Europe, I had never outlined them comprehensively in writing, and nor – come to that – had anyone else. Meanwhile, there was much about the quality of the debate over Europe that I found troubling: it was not so much that the EU was being so roundly denounced in so many quarters, but rather that so much of the denunciation was both wrong-headed and misinformed. Euroscepticism has been on the rise since the early 1990s, but with the euro zone crisis it moved into high gear, and so did the misrepresentations about the power and reach of the EU. Someone clearly needed to step up before veracity was forever sacrificed on the altar of myth. Hence this book.

Before proceeding, a few words of explanation. Because it is the EU that has been the target of so much of the recent analysis and speculation, it might seem that the title of the book should be *Why the European Union Matters*. But integration has always been about more than the work of the EU, or its precursor the European Economic Community. We should not forget the work of the Council of Europe, the European Court of Human Rights, the European Free Trade Association, and a large and diverse community of specialized professional bodies, interest groups and think-tanks working on European matters. We should also not forget the efforts of individuals and groups working outside formal institutions, as well as the effects of broader political, economic and social pressures, such as the cold war, internationalization and globalization. And while the European Union has helped clear the way for the development of a European consciousness, much of what has been achieved has been an accidental rather than a deliberate result of the work of the EU.

With time, there have been two defining trends: Europe and the EU have become conflated, and European integration has developed a momentum and a reach that has carried it beyond the confines of the EU and its member states. Of one thing we can be sure: Europe is more than a body of laws and a network of institutions, and in arguing why Europe matters I am including the ideas and attitudes that together constitute the modern European experience. To avoid distracting semantic logjams, I use the term *Europe* to mean the region as well as the broad process of European integration and cooperation, occasionally use the phrase *European project* to describe the laws, policies, institutions and people involved in that process, and I refer to the European Union when writing specifically about its work.

As for my background, I am a university professor of political science, and have been studying the European Union since the early 1990s, writing about it mainly for students and other academics. I was born in Britain, but I have spent most of my life elsewhere (Kenya, South Africa, Zimbabwe, and now a long-time residency in the United States). I today live a transatlantic existence, carrying British and US passports as I travel back and forth across the Atlantic, but on neither side feeling entirely at home nor entirely foreign. This allows me to look at the both the EU and the US as an insider and an outsider, impressed by the changes I see in Europe, while my views about politics are influenced most immediately by my daily experience of the American model.

I am particularly struck by how often the problems of the European Union are contrasted with the supposed successes of the United States. And yet those of us living west of the Atlantic are reminded on an almost daily basis by commentators, analysts, the media, politicians and other academics of the abundant challenges faced by the United States. These range from a dysfunctional political system to persistent poverty, decaying infrastructure, underachieving schools, incivility in public discourse, institutionalized racism, worrisome social divisions, an expanding gap between rich and poor, unsustainable levels of consumption, a prodigious trade deficit, an addiction to fossil fuels, a permissive gun culture, a byzantine tax code, looming threats to social security and a snowballing national debt.

If there is anyone who is quicker to criticize what they see around them than Europeans, it is Americans. And yet unlike many eurosceptics, who in many cases appear to have thrown in the towel, few in the United States seriously propose giving up or substantially cutting back on the American experiment, and the noun *americscepticism* does not exist. To be fair, the United States is a composite state while the European Union is not, and criticism of the EU is based mainly on arguments in favour of a restoration of state sovereignty. But critics of the US are adept at pointing out what is wrong with their country while also pointing out what is right with it and how the problems might be fixed. Eurosceptics could learn from this.

As an academic, meanwhile, I have been dismayed by how little the work of my peers has entered the public debate about Europe. Academics work hard and publish a great deal, and much of it is fascinating and insightful and even perhaps revolutionary. But the scholarship on Europe is often arcane and theoretical, is rarely read by anyone except other academics, and only infrequently enters the mainstream of political and public debate. This is a problem that is far from unique to the field of European studies, and it is not the sole reason why the EU is misunderstood, but it is unfortunate that so little of this potentially illuminating research should be working its way into the public domain.

While visiting Brussels during 2012 for fieldwork on this book I was struck once again by the contrast between the academic world, with its own vernacular and a dynamic that stops just short of secret handshakes, and my conversations with those in the European institutions and in think-tanks and interest groups who deal with the real and the practical rather than the abstract and the esoteric. As the head of one think-tank explained it to me, academics are usually focused on narrow aspects of policy, which often have nothing to do with the short-term EU agenda. But the problems, she noted, are also partly self-inflicted because academics do not weigh in to contemporary debates through new research, making it difficult for them to have much of a voice in current debates.

My own work has focused on helping university students learn about the EU, and more than once has led to accusations that I paint too positive a picture of my subject, a charge rarely made of anyone writing about national politics in, say, Britain, or Germany, or the United States. Even when a scholar of the EU tries to be neutral it seems that the avoidance of clear and abundant criticism opens them to charges of being too pro-European. In this regard, as in many others, the EU is unique; academics who study and write about it are not only expected to meet the basic requirements of scholarly rigour in their work, but are also closely watched for signs that they are showing too much enthusiasm for the object of their study. I was once even accused by a British eurosceptic of being a traitor to Britain, an incident which finally made me realize just how preposterous some of the turns in the debate about Europe had become.

I have written this book, then, because I believe that Europe matters, that too much of the debate about Europe is poorly informed and misleading, and that we urgently need a better grasp of the longer-term significance of the European experiment. It is not an academic treatise, but is instead written for anyone who wants to better understand the achievements of Europe (and of the European Union in particular), or who needs new support for their pro-European instincts, or has not yet been able to make up their mind. A few eurosceptics might even be encouraged by my arguments into examining Europe from a new perspective.

I owe a debt of gratitude to a number of people who helped both with the development of this book and with shaping the ideas on which it is based. Most immediately, I would like to thank Hubert Zimmermann and Andreas Dür for inviting me to write the short chapter that eventually evolved into this book, and Steven Kennedy for his usual sterling work as my publisher; he has given me excellent advice and encouragement for almost as long as I have been studying the EU, and made numerous suggestions that helped with the final form of this book. My thanks also go to Stephen Wenham for his comments, to Helen Caunce for overseeing the production, to Caroline Richards for her copyediting, and to the staff at Palgrave Macmillan for their fine work.

You often pick up the best ideas in informal conversations, and although most didn't realize it at the time, colleagues in the Erasmus Mundus Euroculture MA with which I have been involved since 2007 have given me many helpful ideas and responses dating back over several years. They include Alexandre Kostka and Terence Boyle of the University of Strasbourg in France; Antonín Kalous of Palacký University in the Czech Republic; Martin Tamcke, Lars Klein and Marc Arwed Rutke of the Georg-August University of Göttingen in Germany; Janny de Jong, Herman Voogsgeerd, Margriet van der Waal and Robert Wagenaar of the University of Groningen in the Netherlands; Claudio Cressati of the University of Udine in Italy; and Asier Altuna of the University of Deusto in Spain. My thanks also to Jorg Monar and Michele Chang at the College of Europe in Bruges, where I was based while the book was in production.

For her comments on the introduction and the chapter on Europe as a global player I would like to thank Mai'a Davis Cross, and for meeting with me to talk about the current state of the European Union, I thank Marc Jorna of the Communication Directorate-General in the European Commission, Marti Grau and his colleagues at the House of European History, Giles Merritt at Friends of Europe, Hans Maartens at the European Policy Centre, Adrian van den Hoven at BusinessEurope, Johannes Keis at BEUC (the European Consumer's Organization), and Gareth Harding. Diogo Pinto at the European Movement International was particularly generous with his insights and his support of the book.

I had the benefit of hosting five visiting European graduate students at my university during the autumn semester of 2012, and exploited them all as a resource. For their help with finding sources and responding to some of my ideas, I thank Alberto Castellanos (from Spain), Katerina Netopilova and Ludmila Vavrova (Czech Republic), Heather Southwood (UK) and Georgios Tsarsitalidis (Greece/Sweden). Three anonymous reviewers commented on my original proposal for the book, and two more commented on an advanced draft, along with John Palmer, and all of them gave me valuable responses that helped tighten and improve my arguments.

And finally, as ever, my thanks and love to Leanne, Ian and Stuart for all the really important things in life.

Map of Europe

Introduction

A day will come when ... you all, nations of the continent, without losing your distinct qualities and your glorious individuality, will be merged closely within a superior unit and you will form the European brotherhood ... A day will come when the only fields of battle will be markets opening up to trade and minds opening up to ideas ... A day will come when we will display cannon in museums just as we display instruments of torture today, and are amazed that such things could ever have been possible.

Victor Hugo, 1849

If Europe were once united in the sharing of its common inheritance, there would be no limit to the happiness, to the prosperity and the glory which its ... people would enjoy.

Winston Churchill, 1946

Europe is a destiny we will never embrace easily. But it ... would be a monumental error of statesmanship to turn our back on it and fall away from a crucial position of power and influence in the 21st Century.

Tony Blair, 2012

At a moving and inspiring ceremony in Oslo on 10 December 2012, leaders of the major institutions of the European Union accepted on behalf of more than 500 million people the award of the Nobel Prize for Peace. The event represented the culmination of more than six decades of hard work aimed at promoting peace and prosperity in a continent that had for centuries been home to some of the world's most intractable and long-lasting conflicts and wars.

In presenting the award, Nobel committee chairman Thorbjoern

Jagland described the reconciliation between France and Germany as 'probably the most dramatic example in history' of war and conflict being turned so rapidly into peace and cooperation. European Council president Herman van Rompuy spoke of the 'bold bet' that Europe's founders had made in breaking the 'endless cycle of violence', and shared his hope that future generations would say with pride 'Ich bin ein Europaer', 'Je suis fier d'etre Europeen', 'I'm proud to be European'. Germany's *Bild* carried a front-page story with the headline 'This prize belongs to us all'. Spain's *El Mundo* recorded that in the chronicles of the European Union, the date of the award ceremony would 'appear in bold and underlined'. It was a day, in short, on which those who believed in the European Union could celebrate its achievements.

And those achievements have been remarkable. As well as having enjoyed the longest spell of general peace in its recorded history, Europe since 1945 has been transformed into a region where political barriers have come down, economic opportunities have been expanded, social priorities have been redefined, cultural differences have been both recognized and celebrated, minds have been opened, horizons have been expanded, and exclusion has been replaced with inclusion. The European Union is the world's wealthiest single market, to which anyone in the world of business craves access. Its work has promoted innovation and choice, underpinned democracy and free markets at home and abroad, reduced regulation and red tape, and encouraged Europeans to focus on what they have in common rather than on what divides them. On the global stage, the EU stands as an exemplar of the moral and political advantages of civilian power, and of the social advantages of investing in schools, hospitals and highways rather than guns, bombs and border guards.

Regrettably, the Oslo ceremony was a rare moment of pride in an era that has seen numerous challenges to the goals that Europe represents. As has been the case with so any other recipients, there were questions about the decision of the Nobel committee to recognize the EU. Some suggested that NATO (North Atlantic Treaty Organization) was at least an equally worthy winner, an argument that rather overlooked the critical point that the EU has always focused on peace through opportunity, cooperation and the rule of law, while NATO is a military alliance that keeps peace mainly by threatening violence against anyone who might undermine that peace. Doubters also questioned the timing of the award, presented against a background of crisis in the euro zone and a sorry tale of austerity and high unemployment. The resulting tensions, some suggested, might be causing Europe to turn back from the path of peace and cooperation. The award, said others, had come as euro zone governments were showing a distinct lack of goodwill towards one another, and bickering over how the debt crisis might best be resolved. But, it should be pointed out, at least they were bickering peacefully.

The contrasting visions of celebration and doubt, of achievement and stress, of pride and criticism, speak volumes about the current state of the debate about Europe. Efforts to integrate the region have long had their doubters and critics, but at no time have the dismissals been more voluble or the predictions of doom so numerous as since the advent in 2009 of the sovereign debt crisis in the euro zone. What at first seemed to be mainly a domestic policy problem for Greece soon took on deeper and wider significance, leading to the breaking of a floodwall of alarm as concerns about the stability of the euro spilled over into doubts about the entire future of European integration.

But while there is undoubtedly much that is wrong with Europe, there is far more that is right with it. And contrary to what we are often told, Europeans support its work, often by large margins. Even as the problems of the euro worsened in early 2011, those who thought positively about the EU outnumbered those who thought negatively by two to one, and those who were optimistic for its future outnumbered the pessimists by nearly six to four.[1] As the crisis deepened during 2012, more than half of Europeans remained in favour of a common economic and monetary system while only 40 per cent were opposed. And rather than the crisis sparking a mass rejection of Europe as pessimists might have expected, most Europeans believed that EU countries would need to work more closely together in the wake of the crisis, and that the EU would be stronger as a result of it.[2]

There is an old adage that out of crisis comes opportunity. Even if Europe today faces many challenges, they stand as the greatest opportunity in the history of the EU to learn, reconsider and embark on a voyage of constructive reform. But it will be hard to make progress so long as the debate over Europe is flawed and distracted, and there are many such flaws and distractions at work today, which have encouraged Europeans to look the other way while the baby hovers dangerously close to being thrown out with the bathwater.

Prime among those distractions is the pessimism that attends most of the assessments of Europe's possibilities. Almost from the day of its birth, but certainly from the advent of its first major crises in the 1960s, alarmists have declared European integration to be variously dead, dying or comatose. Few have done this so persistently as *The Economist*, whose cover designers have apparently been engaged of late in a contest to outdo themselves in the wittiness of their predictions of collapse in the euro zone. A May 2010 cover was particularly perverse, with its headline 'Acropolis Now' and a glum-looking Angela Merkel uttering the words 'The horror, the horror'.

But wind the clock back to 1982 and we find the same newspaper with a cover showing a tombstone bearing the words 'EEC: Born March 25 1957, Moribund March 25 1982' and adapting the judgement of the historian Tacitus on the Roman Emperor Galba: *Capax imperii nisi imperasset* (It seemed capable of being a power until it tried to be one). The editors bemoaned ineffectual leadership from the Commission, a disappointing European Parliament, an indecisive Council of Ministers, apathetic public opinion, an economic slump in western Europe, and the need for Europe's leaders to find the vision needed to address its disagreements.[3] More than 30 years later they offer almost the same complaints, which made it all the more ironic to see *The Economist* in late 2012 regretting the growing prospect of Britain leaving the EU, an eventuality that it had helped create.

So much has the gloom become received wisdom that an exasperated José Manuel Barroso, president of the European Commission, was prompted not long ago to note the 'intellectual glamour of pessimism and constant denigration' that was doing so much harm to Europe's image.[4] Of course there have been problems, which were both inevitable and predictable; European integration has always, after all, been an ambitious and complex scheme that even today continues to chart new territory. And the EU is hardly alone in facing difficulties and challenges, which are the stuff of public debate in every state and society in the world. But while most of those states and societies work to fix their problems, the pessimism about Europe has gone untreated for so long that it has progressed into a severe bout of success denial. For every suggestion that Europe has made progress or notched up an achievement there is usually a 'Yes, but ...' response driven by an unwillingness to give the EU credit even when such credit is abundantly due.

The second distraction in the debate about Europe is the lack of political courage on the part of Europe's leaders. Without much in the way of a road map or an agreed destination, they have moved ahead in fits and starts, muddling through, making decisions on the fly, worrying often about not being seen to be too European for fear of sparking a nationalist backlash. But as the MEP Andrew Duff reminds us, 'the EU was and still is experimental', and it has always been unwise to believe that it was 'condemned to succeed'.[5] It is also worth noting that many of its problems are less the result of European integration having gone too far than of it not having gone far enough. Critics like to argue that integration has created burdensome new regulations and impinged too much on national sovereignty, but we are told at the same time by business leaders, consumer organizations, environmentalists, educationists, economists and defence analysts that there are too many remaining gaps in the structure of integration and that what we really need is more Europe, not less Europe. It reminds one of the joke about the country that decided to switch from driving on one side of the road to the other, but in order to ease the stress on drivers it was agreed to make the change in stages.

The final and most troublesome distraction in the debate over Europe is the swelling chorus of euroscepticism, or – perhaps more accurately – of EU-scepticism. Judicious and informed criticism of Europe is, of course, a legitimate and essential part of the debate, but there is an unhappy tradition of misrepresenting the work of the EU for political ends, routinely painting it in an unflattering light, dismissing it for shortcomings of the kind that apply at least equally to its member states, greatly exaggerating the reach and powers of the European institutions, and using Europe as a handy scapegoat for problems that have entirely separate origins. The more impulsive eurosceptics even talk of a conspiracy to defraud Europe's states of their sovereignty by means of subterfuge and intrigue.[6] The effect has been to shroud the debate over Europe in a fog of myth and misunderstanding. Europhiles, meanwhile, have not spoken up as forcefully as they might have, with the result that the eurosceptic view has earned a presence out of all proportion to the number of its sympathizers.

A brief explanatory aside is in order. The popular use of the term *euroscepticism* to describe opposition to the European project gives the false impression that there is a monolithic and consistent set of anti-European (or anti-EU) sentiments. In truth, there are multiple shades of critical opinion that vary by time, place, depth and political persuasion. A distinction needs to be made between soft scepticism (qualified opposition to the direction being taken by integration) and hard scepticism (a belief that integration is fundamentally wrong and needs to be abandoned).[7] A distinction also needs to be made between diffuse opinions about European integration and more specific opinions about the EU itself;[8] it is possible, in other words, to support integration in principle while being critical of the institutional design and the particular policies of the EU.

The term *eurosceptic* is thought to have entered the political lexicon in Britain in the mid-1980s,[9] ironically just as the single market programme was set to draw new and mainly positive attention to Europe. As integration picked up speed and expanded its reach with the Maastricht Treaty (signed in February 1992), more Europeans began to feel its effects, and opinion hardened; Maastricht pushed integration beyond the single market, and raised troubling questions about the implications for national sovereignty. Three critical events came later that year: the Danish vote against Maastricht on 2 June, the Black Wednesday crisis of 16 September when Britain was obliged to withdraw from early efforts to create the foundations for a single European currency, and the approval of Maastricht in France by a whisker four days later.

Where once euroscepticism had been mainly a British phenomenon, it now entered the political debate in almost every EU member state, spawning political parties opposed to European integration, generating pro- and anti-European splits within existing parties, and influencing thinking on everything from treaty reforms and enlargement to new policy initiatives. Critical opinions have since hardened in the wake of the euro zone crisis, the mainstream thinking coalescing around three broad charges:

- Integration threatens national sovereignty by impinging upon the powers of member states to make law and policy, the biggest concern being that the EU is headed down the dangerous path to becoming a federal European superstate at the expense of the self-determination of its member states. There are concerns, too, about what integration means for national identity.

- The EU institutions are undemocratic and elitist, and insufficiently open or responsive to the opinions of the citizens of the member states. Criticism is directed particularly at the European Commission for being unelected while also having the authority to draft new EU laws and oversee their implementation.

- Integration is inefficient, in that instead of opening up the marketplace and expanding the range of economic opportunities available to Europeans, it has meant a greater regulatory burden. Harmonization has reduced the ability of national governments to respond to the distinctive economic problems of their countries, and does not take sufficient account of national policy needs and differences.

Adding to these general concerns, there are varieties of euroscepticism peculiar to individual member states, and even to parties or political groups within those states. So while the French left criticizes the EU for its elitism and its association with globalization, the French right worries about the threat it poses to national identity, and the far right sees integration as signalling 'the end of France, the French people, its language and its culture'.[10] In Germany, meanwhile, euroscepticism is both more muted and of more recent origin; unsubstantiated fears that a combination of greater competition and enlargement might compromise Germany's economic success by adversely affecting jobs, wages and social standards[11] have since been heightened by resentment at having to bail out misbehaving members of the euro zone. And in multiple EU states we have the paradox of open borders feeding into a reaction against immigration that has fuelled the often strident anti-EU warnings of extreme right-wing political parties and movements.

To summarize, then, we find the discussion about Europe mired in a toxic stew of pessimism, denial, hesitancy, myth and scepticism. It is hard to think of a public debate that has been both so consequential and yet also so abundantly plagued by misinformation. It is also hard to think of one where there has been such a conspicuous gap between the supportive sentiments of so many ordinary people and the critical positions of so many opinion leaders. If there is a single root cause, it is the knowledge deficit, or the gap between what the EU does and what most Europeans know and understand about its work. The problem of the uninformed citizen is nothing new, nor is it unique to the EU; there is an extensive body of research dating back decades that confirms how little most people know about most public issues.[12] But few initiatives have suffered quite so abundantly from confusion and uncertainty as the European Union.

There is a view in the academic world that we need not worry. Researchers tell us that as levels of knowledge about an issue fall, we rely on experts – including the media, political leaders, political parties and interest groups – to fill in the gaps by offering us cues.[13] But other researchers tell us that even the experts can make mistakes, will rarely admit them, and can be blindsided by events.[14] They are, furthermore, often bad at predicting outcomes because of their poor understanding of probability and uncertainty,[15] and will often be driven in their analyses by narrow political agendas. As the audience for those analyses, we can do little more than decide which we find the most instinctively compelling, or which fit best with our own knowledge and direct experience. But when it comes to understanding something as unusual, as complex and as unpredictable as the European Union, the challenges grow exponentially.

The euro zone crisis is a case in point. Many of the brightest and the best have applied themselves to resolving the problem, but while there is a consensus that the euro had design flaws from the beginning (some avoidable, others unanticipated), the uncertainty over how to respond, coupled with concerns about what would be acceptable to voters, went on to generate talk of a wild variety of possible futures. The lack of certainty was nicely encapsulated in two articles that appeared in different issues of the journal *Foreign Affairs* during 2012. In the first, a Harvard economist boldly declared that the euro had failed, along with 'the political goal of creating a harmonious Europe', and that it had been a death foretold.[16] In the second, another leading economist insisted that predictions of the euro's collapse were 'vastly overblown', and that if history was any guide, Europe would 'emerge from its current turmoil not only with the euro intact but also with stronger institutions and far better economic prospects for the future'.[17]

This book is a response to the scepticism and the doubts about Europe. In the chapters that follow, I set out to show how and why

Europe matters and to make the particular case for the European Union. I argue that integration has been good for Europe and for the rest of the world, and I show how and why this is so. I also argue that integration has given us a new way of doing political, economic and social business that is more peaceful and productive than anything its member states could achieve in isolation, and that it has welcome implications not just for Europe but for the rest of the world.

I focus on how European integration has improved life in real and tangible ways for real people, and also on how it has brought deeper changes that are not always immediately obvious. I offer counterfactuals by speculating about what life might have been like without European cooperation, and might be like for member states that leave. I also address the most dangerous and persistent myths in the debate about Europe, showing how the debate has been undermined by false allegations. Finally, I offer suggestions on where Europe might go from here. It is quite different from what it was 10 or 20 years ago, and doubtless will be quite different 10 or 20 years hence. I will argue that we today have the opportunity to embark on a programme of informed and sensible reform, and that the most desirable option is a reordering based on recognizing the EU as a confederal union of states, albeit with some federal qualities.

My central arguments can be summarized thus:

- The debate about Europe can be fruitful only if we have a better understanding of the EU and the process of integration, unclouded by myth.
- Integration has helped mould Europe into a peaceful and peace-making example in a world where many retain an unhealthy fascination with military power.
- Europe abundantly illustrates the benefits of free trade and of carefully reducing the barriers to the free movement of people, money, goods and services. Once the problems of the euro are resolved (as they will be), we will better appreciate the benefits and advantages of a single currency.
- There is majority support for integration among Europeans, and numerous channels through which their interests are represented and protected. While democracy is messy and imperfect, talk of a European-level democratic deficit is exaggerated.

- There is a community of Europe that is easier to define than most people believe, and Europeans have much more in common than most of them realize.
- The European political model has encouraged compromise, consensus, higher standards and improved protection, and is an effective means to the resolution of shared problems.
- The EU stands as an exemplar of a global player that uses inclusive and soft tools to achieve its policy objectives.
- We need an improved Europe, meaning that we need to build on those areas where integration works, repair those that do not, fill in the gaps, and make sure that Europe is better understood.

It is one thing to give up on a project because it is not working, but quite another to throw in the towel having never really understood what we were doing or where we were headed. It is time to turn down the volume on the eurosceptics, to look at Europe more carefully, to give credit where it is due, to fix the problems, and to make decisions on the basis of an informed and carefully considered understanding of what Europe means. Thanks mainly to integration, Europe is more peaceful, prosperous and positively influential than it has ever been in its history; it could achieve even more if we were to take care of its many items of unfinished business; and it is in the interests of Europe and the wider world that we understand this and build upon the achievements.

1 What Is Europe?

The debate about Europe suffers from a single, acute handicap: most people know little about how the European Union works, and most of the rest cannot agree on what it is or what it might become. There are many opinions but few hard certainties, and the result has been a turmoil of confusion and misrepresentation, begging the obvious question of how we can have an informed or productive exchange without understanding just what we are discussing. It is much like the Indian parable of the group of blind people who try to determine what an elephant looks like by touching it and then comparing notes; how we understand the EU depends on how we look at it, how we define its work, and our points of comparison.

Even those best placed to help us understand – the university scholars who base their careers on studying and explaining the EU – have stumbled. In their well-meaning efforts to pin down its character, they have offered such uncongenial labels as *multi-level governance*, *consociationalism* and *quasi-federal polity*, to each of which other scholars have been quick to offer strings of objections. Many have avoided the question altogether by describing the EU as *sui generis* (unique) before moving on to other conversations. Even Jacques Delors, former president of the European Commission, had to concede that the EU was an 'unidentified political object'.

But a Chinese proverb tells us that the beginning of wisdom is to call things by their right name, and what we think of Europe depends very much on how we brand it. Today's EU began life in 1952 as a slightly unusual international organization with six members whose interests were defined and defended by their national governments with little public involvement. It then evolved in 1958 into a more ambitious effort to build a European single market, but was still an international organization in which most Europeans took little interest. It was only with the passage in 1992 of the Treaty on European Union (otherwise known as the Maastricht Treaty) that the debate

11

moved into a higher gear with concerns that new efforts were being made to build a federal United States of Europe, which had always been the goal of the most committed Europeanists.

While the new European Union still had some of the qualities of a standard international organization, it had accumulated treaties, permanent administrative institutions, an expanding body of law, a court that interpreted the treaties, and a directly elected Parliament. Critics charged that this amounted to a new level of government with independent powers and a troubling desire to nibble away at the sovereignty of its member states. A backlash began, euroscepticism accelerated, and alarm bells began ringing more stridently in 2009 as the curtain went up on the Greek sovereign debt crisis.

There had already been plenty of European crises, including the collapse of an ambitious French-led effort to create a European Defence Community in 1954, Charles de Gaulle's unilateral dismissal of two British applications to join the European Economic Community in the 1960s, and the failure in the early 1970s of efforts to create a European single currency. A troubled Jean Monnet, one of the founding fathers of Europe, was prompted to warn in his 1978 memoirs that 'Europe would be built through crises' and would be 'the sum of their solutions'.[1] He also introduced what came to be known as Monnet's law: 'people only accept change when they are faced with necessity, and only recognize necessity when a crisis is upon them'.[2]

More crises followed Monnet's warning, including repeated problems with plans for the single currency and surprise national votes against new EU treaties, but the euro zone crisis was clearly the most serious of them all. Having failed to meet the terms of membership, Greece should not have been allowed to join the euro, but even Germany and France rode roughshod over the rules they had themselves designed to keep the euro stable. And while the euro had design flaws, it also suffered pressures from the global financial crisis of 2007–10, years of economic mismanagement in Greece, and a debt-fuelled boom in southern Europe. But its problems illustrated a wider and more fundamental point: even after more than 60 years of efforts to integrate Europe, remarkably little was understood about the character, needs, effects, functioning or possibilities of integration.

Fanned by the winds of the euro zone crisis, the flames of the debate about Europe have never burned brighter than they do today, but the uncertainties continue unabated. They are reflected in the wide range of scenarios that have been suggested, which run the gamut from some light strategic tinkering to the creation of a two-speed Europe, an accelerated drive towards a federal Europe, tactical exits by more eurosceptic states such as Britain, or perhaps even the collapse of the entire endeavour in an atmosphere of bitterness and recrimination. Wilder voices have even suggested that the end of the euro might mean the erosion of democracy, the collapse of the European social and economic model, a new German domination, and a return to political conflict and extremism.[3] In all the uproar, the voices of scepticism and dismissal have become louder, and reminders of the positives that Europe has brought have become harder to find.

Before getting to grips with the advantages and achievements of the EU, then, we need first to be clear about what it is and how it works, which means a brief review of the work of the European institutions. We need to pay particular attention to the European Commission, the one institution most often derided by eurosceptics for myriad and usually imaginary misdemeanours. We also need to address the knotty question of how best to understand the political personality of the EU, and for this we already have a handy term available that is all but ignored in the debate over Europe: *confederation*, meaning a union of states that works together on matters of mutual interest but remains at heart a club of member states rather than a system of government in its own right. The EU has some federal qualities, to be sure, but for now at least it is best regarded as a looser confederal arrangement.

Understanding Europe

When it comes to large-scale political organization, the most common unit of administration is the state. The world is divided up into nearly 200 of them, their core features being a territory, a population, sovereignty, a government, legitimacy and independence. But no state is truly independent, because each is bound to others by political, economic and social ties; they share critical resources (such as energy, minerals, water supplies and clean air); and they routinely cooperate with each other (or abuse each other) in the meeting rooms of international organizations. The state has its advantages, including the institutions it provides by which its residents govern themselves, make laws, manage economies, deal with other states, and ensure public safety and national security. States also give people a sense of belonging and identity. However, they are also far from perfect:

- They impose artificial political divisions on human society, encouraging people to pursue narrow and sometimes imagined interests at the expense of broader welfare. At worst, state-driven patriotism and nationalism can encourage a sense of superiority, exclusivity and distrust.
- They have borders that impede the free movement of people, money, ideas, goods and services, and while this sometimes makes organizational sense it can also handicap economic and social development.
- Their efforts to guarantee the security of their citizens has often encouraged them to use threats and intimidation against other states, the resulting tensions occasionally leading to conflict and war.
- They have often done a poor job of working together to address shared problems such as terrorism, trans-boundary pollution, illegal immigration and the spread of disease.
- They have often been unable to meet the demands of their residents for justice, prosperity and human rights, or to manage their economies and natural resources to the benefit of all their residents. Their democratic records have been mixed, and even the wealthiest and most progressive of states still often struggle with poverty and social division.
- States often oblige people with different national, racial, religious, political and economic backgrounds to live together in tense and artificial political arrangements rather than being allowed independence and self-determination.

States have also not been with us that long. We were almost all born and raised with them, and thus can be forgiven for thinking of most of them as ancient and venerable, but the modern state system has roots that go back only to the early modern era (roughly the 1600s), and most states are recent creations: nearly 80 per cent were formed during the twentieth century. So there is little that is either permanent or enduring about the state, and even today large question marks hang over the future of Britain, Belgium, Spain and other European states with active independence or secessionist movements. Adding to their problems and weaknesses, the place of states in the global system has been altered since 1945 by two key developments.

First, there has been a new focus on international cooperation in response to the growth in political and economic interdependence. This is reflected in the signing of treaties and the rise of international organizations based on voluntary cooperation, communal management and shared interests. There were no more than a few hundred of these bodies in existence before the Second World War, but thousands more have since been created, ranging from large intergovernmental bodies whose members are states (the United Nations, the World Trade Organization, the North Atlantic Treaty Organization and so on) to non-governmental organizations such as Amnesty International and the International Red Cross, and multinational corporations such as Ford, Toyota, BP, ING, Allianz and HSBC. Their number and their power have combined to reduce the reach and independence of states, and their existence has made cooperation on shared needs and problems quite normal.

Second, there has been the spread of globalization, or the process by which politics, economics, culture, technology and the provision of services have been blended across state borders. Never before has the degree of such blending been so great as it is today, or the daily lives of so many people been so impacted by decisions taken in other states and on other continents. We trade with one another, jobs have been outsourced, multinational corporations make many of the decisions once restricted to governments, technology places us in almost instant touch with developments all over the world, we can be immediately impacted by events in other countries, and – for the global middle class at least – homes are full of goods made all over the world, and international travel has become routine. Where states were once the masters of markets, argues Susan Strange, the roles have in many respects been reversed.[4]

The European Union works at the confluence of states and international organizations, so it is important to make a distinction between its intergovernmental and supranational qualities: in other words, how much is it still a club of states and how much is it a new level of government with powers and authority of its own? The short answer: it is more the former than the latter. The parent of today's EU was the European Coal and Steel Community (ECSC), founded in 1952 with an appointed High Authority charged with removing barriers to free trade in coal and steel, and an appointed Court of Justice that could rule on disputes. Both were supranational in character, meaning that they worked above the level of the member states, and with the broader interest of their six member states in mind. But real power to make decisions rested with the Council of Ministers, which was intergovernmental in the sense that it was where government representatives from the member states could negotiate with one another and could protect national interests.

This formula was passed on in 1958 to the European Economic Community (EEC), which had an appointed Commission, an appointed European Court of Justice, and a weak and unelected European Parliament. The focus of decision making lay with the Council of Ministers, where national interests continued to be defended by permanent representatives and government ministers, the latter taking votes on all new legislative proposals. Few Europeans paid much heed to the work of the EEC, and few of those who did had much cause to worry that national interests were not being protected by their home governments. Those interests were again to the fore in the 1970s with the creation of a new institution – the European Council – within which the heads of government of the member states meet to make the broad, strategic decisions on integration. Table 1 gives an overview of the EU system.

What we have in today's EU, then, is the following:

- A *European Council* made up of the heads of government of the member states, that acts as something of a steering committee or board of directors for the EU, and where the interests of the member states are very much on show.
- A *European Commission* whose leaders (the commissioners) are appointed by the governments of the member states; it has the power only to propose and dispose (it cannot make decisions on new laws and policies, only draft them and oversee their execution), and is charged with serving the needs of the member states in areas defined and limited by the treaties.

Table 1   A guide to the EU institutions

Institution	Membership	Character	Function
European Council	Elected heads of government of the member states, overseen by an appointed president	Intergovernmental	A steering committee charged with making broad decisions on the process of integration
European Commission	Commissioners nominated by national governments, overseeing 40,000 career bureaucrats	Supranational	Proposes new laws and policies, and oversees their execution once enacted by the Council of the EU and Parliament
Council of the European Union	Government ministers from the member states	Intergovernmental	Shares power with Parliament over the enactment of proposals for new laws
European Parliament	Elected representatives from the member states	Supranational	Shares power with the Council of the EU over the enactment of proposals for new laws
European Court of Justice	Judges appointed by the member states	Supranational	Ensures that the actions of individuals, organizations and governments fit with the terms of the treaties

- A *Council of the European Union* where permanent representatives of the member states vet all proposals for new laws before passing them on to the national government ministers, who share powers with the European Parliament on final enactment.
- A *European Parliament* whose members are elected every five years in competitive elections, who represent voter interests, and

who have the power to amend new laws and share – with the Council of the EU – the power to make final decisions.

- A *European Court of Justice* whose judges are appointed by the member states and whose job is to make sure that everyone behaves themselves by not overstepping the terms of the treaties.

In short, the EU is an organization whose work is in the hands of institutions whose members are either elected by European voters, appointed by national governments, or are drawn directly from those national governments. So while we can say that the EU is more than a conventional international organization, and while there has been much pooling or sharing of policy responsibilities, the EU falls some way short of being a federal United States of Europe, and – most importantly – there is direct or indirect accountability to European voters all along the way. That Brussels has somehow accumulated independent powers and has the ability to make decisions without the input of national governments or their representatives is one of the great enduring fictions about Europe. Thus when Nigel Farage, leader of the UK Independence Party, charged in 2012 that the outcome of the next general election in Britain was moot because 'we are not governed from Westminster, we are governed from Brussels'[5], it was an overstatement bordering on the delirious.

We also need to understand the broader pressures that encourage states to cooperate even outside the hallways of international organizations or bodies such as the EU. When Adam Smith, the father of capitalism, wrote in *The Wealth of Nations* against the government regulation of markets, he pointed out how individuals looking only for self-interest and security could end up being led by an 'invisible hand' to promote the broader interests of society. This notion of the invisible hand has since been interpreted in different ways, the economist Milton Friedman, for example, writing of its role in encouraging 'the possibility of cooperation without coercion'.[6] In the case of cooperation among states as closely intertwined as those in Europe, the invisible hand of the marketplace would doubtless have led European states to cooperate even if organizations like the EU had never been invented. All the more reason, then, why the debate about Europe must go beyond the EU and include the whole array of political, economic and social pressures that encourage cooperation, and that inform the work of the Council of Europe and the wider community of specialized European cooperative bodies and interest groups.

Addressing the Myths

The unusual and even often unique organizational qualities of the EU – and our unfortunate difficulties in agreeing just what it is or what it should be – has left us with a situation in which much of the political and media analysis of the EU is confused, sometimes wrong, and often misleading. This has paved the way for a cottage industry devoted to the production and promotion of myths about the EU, which have in turn come to exert a malign influence on the way the EU is (mis)understood. These myths fall mainly into six parts.

First, the European project is often charged with being elitist; in other words, it is described as being under the control of those small groups of people who – by virtue of their wealth, education, abilities or offices – enjoy a disproportionate level of influence in the societies of which they are part. We are talking here mainly about political and party leaders, business leaders, the media, academics and interest groups. *The Economist* has described both the euro and the European Central Bank as 'elite projects *par excellence*', commenting on the manner in which 'the high priests of Europe's political class handed down the edict that Europe needed its own currency' in the 1990s.[7] Even the normally pro-European philosopher Jürgen Habermas commented in 2011 on how political elites were 'burying their heads in the sand' and 'doggedly persisting with their elitist project and the disenfranchisement of the European population'.[8] The charge of elitism has been one of the sparks behind the rise of populist parties in Europe in recent years.

But while two wrongs do not make a right, the EU is no more or less elitist than national systems of administration, and indeed its very elitism derives from the national cultures out of which it was born and by which it has since been sustained. Elites function at the national level just as much as at the EU level, and many continue to do double duty at both levels, since several of the core European institutions consist of senior members of national governments. This presents us with the interesting picture of national elites accusing the EU of being too elitist. Furthermore, there are plenty of channels

---

Box 1: Six myths about the European project

1. It is elitist.
2. The EU institutions have become too powerful and lack transparency.
3. The EU institutions are unusually inefficient.
4. Anti-European sentiment is widespread and growing.
5. Integration is leading to a loss of national sovereignty.
6. Integration has greatly increased the regulatory burden on the EU member states.

---

through which Europeans can engage directly in the work of the EU, but which most have chosen to ignore, thereby exacerbating the EU's elitist qualities. Consider, for example, the elections to the European Parliament upon which European voters have been turning their backs in growing numbers.

Second, the EU institutions are accused of having become too powerful, and for taking too many decisions behind closed doors with inadequate reference to citizens. But they have minimal independent powers and can mainly do only as much as the member states or the treaties allow them to do; they are either the servants of the member states (the Commission), the servants of the treaties (the Court of Justice), the elected representatives of EU voters (the European Parliament) or government representatives from the member states (the European Council and the Council of the EU), and they are all held accountable to the terms of the treaties. And they are often more open and transparent than their national equivalents, going to great pains to make their work public.

If anyone is to blame for taking decisions behind closed doors it is those national leaders who choose not to put European questions to the test of public opinion, usually because they fear that it will be hostile. And even when Europeans are invited to participate more directly in EU decision making, as they are every five years with elections to the European Parliament, or in more infrequent national referendums, they often either neglect the opportunity by not turning out, or vote on the basis of issues only tangentially related to the question at stake. There is, in short, plenty of democracy and accountability to go around, but few European voters avail themselves of it.

Third, the EU institutions are criticized for their inefficiency. They can be difficult to understand, to be sure, but this is less because efforts are being made to conceal and dissemble than because their structure is the cumulative result of more than 60 years of negotiations aimed at achieving a consensus in the face of conflicting views and demands. If a camel is a horse designed by a committee, then the EU is a set of institutions designed as a result of decades of rearguard actions fought in the interests of the member states. The product is not always pretty, but all large organizations face problems in their design and operation,[9] and the EU institutions have many of the same disadvantages as any network of large organizations: being governed by the self-preservation and self-justification of their administrators and staff, falling victim to changed circumstances and unexpected challenges, and being subject to the different levels of energy, motivation, cooperation, understanding and intelligence that their employees bring to their jobs.

Fourth, there is a misconception that anti-European sentiment is widespread and growing. Thus the political scientist Simon Hix, in his book *What's Wrong with the European Union and How to Fix It*, premises much of his argument on 'the dramatic collapse in the popular legitimacy of the EU since the early 1990s' and its 'worryingly low levels of popular support'.[10] But while levels of support have certainly taken a hammering in the wake of the euro zone crisis, those who believe that membership of the EU has benefited their country consistently outnumber those who do not (often by a factor of two to one), those who have a positive image of the EU have outnumbered those who have a negative image by as much as three to one, and optimists for the future of the EU greatly outnumbered pessimists even as late as 2011. There is more detail about this in Chapter 4, the evidence of widespread popular support for the EU being so compelling that eurosceptics could be forgiven for having many sleepless nights.

Fifth, there is a widespread assumption that integration is leading to a loss of national sovereignty. There is no question that authority in selected policy responsibilities has been pooled and that harmonization has reduced the number of policy areas in which EU member states can operate independently, but much of this would

Document 1: EU mythology at work

An example of the manner in which myths about Europe are created and perpetuated is offered by the web site of the eurosceptic British interest group Civitas. In a fact sheet headed 'Arguments against the EU'[11] it asserts that the EU is undemocratic – but how does the evidence it offers hold up? My responses are in italics.

'The European Union has a lot of power [*it has little independent power*] but is much less accountable to the people than national governments [*directly accountable, yes, but indirectly accountable, no*]. Most EU decisions are made [*abundantly untrue*] or shaped [*partly true*] by the EU Commission which is led by unelected Commissioners [*true, but they are appointed by elected national leaders, just as national ministers are appointed by heads of government. And there is resistance among anti-Europeans to the idea of arranging elections for Commissioners*] and run by an appointed bureaucracy [*true, just like national bureaucracies*].

The democratic element of the EU model – the European Parliament – has fewer powers than a national legislature [*true, but only because national legislatures do not want to surrender more powers*] and rarely influences EU decisions [*abundantly untrue; Parliament shares powers with the Council of the EU on changing, accepting or rejecting every proposal for a new EU law*]. Turnout at European Parliament elections is so low that it is difficult to proclaim its legitimacy [*Parliament is less legitimate because voters choose not to take part in EP elections? A deeply flawed logic*].

The other key decision-making body – the European Council – is secretive [*much like national cabinets*], often meeting behind closed doors to thrash out deals [*again like national cabinets, and Council members are elected national leaders who are accountable to their voters, plus the results of Council deliberations are made public*]. All of this demonstrates contempt for democracy [*national leaders designed the institutions of the EU and decided how much power they should or should not have, so surely they are the ones showing contempt*] and a reluctance to engage with voters [*or is it the voters who are reluctant to engage with the EU institutions?*].'

have happened without the intermediary of the European Union, if only because of the wider pressures of globalization. And much of the 'loss' has come at the benefit of improvements in policy options: removing retrograde barriers to trade, eliminating overlap and duplication, encouraging laggard states to rise to the standards of more progressive neighbours, closing legislative and policy gaps, sharing and pooling knowledge, increasing competition and reducing prices. And even if we could somehow stop the process of European integration, or if a member state were to leave, it is unlikely that much of the independence 'lost' would, could or – for purposes of efficiency – should be restored, because integration has focused mainly on policies where cross-border cooperation has made the most sense.

Some eurosceptics might wish fervently that their country could leave the EU, but they would still find themselves outside the EU cooperating on similar matters and in a similar manner to those required by membership of the EU. We have only to look at the examples of Iceland, Norway and Switzerland – the longest western European hold-outs against membership of the EU – to see how the economic pressures and opportunities of ties to the EU marketplace have encouraged them to change laws and policies to fit. Unfortunately for them, they have had to adopt many of the features of EU law and policy without being full voting members of the club. There are payoffs in the sense that these countries can take better advantage of the opportunities offered by the EU without committing to membership, but the cost is that the changes come without these countries having a direct say in the matter. As one columnist wryly notes, 'Norway simply takes the EU's instructions off the fax machine and implements them.'[12]

Finally, one of the most popular myths directed at the EU is that it has increased the regulatory burden on its member states, not only reducing the powers of national legislatures along the way, but also interfering with the functioning of the free market. Critics suggest that as many as four out of five national laws are prompted by the requirements of EU law. However, the data do not bear this out. Not only is it difficult to be sure about how many EU laws are active at any given time, but their effects vary, they are transposed and implemented differently, they have different levels of impact on different member states, and we should not forget that many of them offer a rationalization that results in fewer barriers and greater efficiency.

Probably fewer than 15 per cent of national laws in the more democratic western European states have been the result of EU requirements. (There is more about this in Chapter 6.)

None of the major EU institutions has been so strenuously criticized, or has been the subject of quite such creative mythology, as the European Commission. It is the bureaucracy of the EU, and as such fits the standard definition of bureaucracies everywhere: large organizations staffed by non-elected officials charged with executing rules and laws. It has two jobs: first, to turn the general goals of the treaties into proposals for new policies and laws, and then to oversee the execution of these policies and laws through the member states (it has no direct powers of enforcement). The Commission is repeatedly charged by sceptics with being large, powerful, unelected, opaque and a waste of money, but few of the criticisms hold up.

- It is not unusually large. It has a staff of about 40,000, of whom about one-third work in translation or interpretation services. This means that there are fewer than 27,000 full-blown Eurocrats to service an EU population of more than half a billion people, a ratio of one Commission staff member per 19,000 residents of the EU. By contrast, Britain has just short of half a million civil servants,[13] or one per 120 Britons, or 158 times as many as the Commission on a per capita basis. And most of those who work in the Commission are talented operators, employed as a result of a stringent and competitive selection procedure, speaking multiple languages, often working long hours to turn broad goals into specific laws, and generally giving the European taxpayer good value for money. The Commission is so small relative to the size of its job, in fact, that it must rely on interest groups and private individuals to help it monitor the implementation of EU law in the member states.
- It is not particularly powerful. As we have seen, while the Commission proposes it is the Council of the EU and the European Parliament that dispose by making the final decision on the enactment of new laws. The Commission also goes to great lengths to include interested parties in early discussions about new laws and policies, is limited in what it can do by the treaties, and is held accountable for many of its actions by

Parliament and the Council of the EU. National senior bureaucrats can become more powerful than their political bosses because they have spent years developing their careers and have superior access to information and policy networks, while ministers come and go. By contrast, the leadership of the Commission has so many legal and functional restrictions on its work, and so much turnover, that it is distinctly less powerful and influential than its national counterparts. Indeed, if there is anything for which presidents of the Commission are criticized more often than their power, it is their weakness and their lack of leadership.

- It is unelected, to be sure, but then so is every standard bureaucracy in the world, from the national to the local. All are staffed and managed by unelected career bureaucrats whose formal accountability is upwards to elected government leaders rather than downwards to voters. The leaders of the Commission – the commissioners who manage its work – are nominated by the governments of the member states, who are in turn elected by the voters of their respective states, thereby providing the same indirect democratic control over the Commission as is the case with national bureaucracies. It is particularly odd to see the Commission being criticized for lacking a quality that is quite usual – and rarely questioned – in national bureaucracies.

- It is not unusually opaque, and certainly no more so than most national bureaucracies. It makes considerable efforts to provide information on its work and its agenda – certainly as much as, if not more than, standard national government departments. Its web site, for example, has information on its structure, the work of its administrators, its key policy areas, its agenda and its budget, and includes a listing of almost the entire body of law that the EU has adopted or is considering. This is more than can be said for the average national bureaucracy.

- It is not particularly expensive. Annual spending on administration for the EU institutions in the most recent budgetary cycle comes to about six per cent of the EU budget, or about €8 billion, which is equivalent to 16 cents for every man, woman and child in the EU. Of that, the Commission accounts for nearly half, or about €3.6 billion (excluding pensions).[14] This figure covers salaries, expenses, travel, buildings and resources, and while there are plenty of examples of budgetary waste and mismanagement in the Commission, the same could be said of almost every bureaucracy.

By way of comparison, Britain's National Health Service (NHS) employs 1.7 million people, of whom more than half are not clinically qualified. While precise figures on the costs of NHS administration are not always easy to find (because the government is reluctant to release them), a House of Commons committee in 2010 revealed that about 14 per cent of NHS spending went on administration. With a €132 billion budget in 2011–12, that worked out at just over €300 for every man, woman and child in the UK.[15] So this was just one (albeit large) government programme in just one EU member state, spending nearly 1900 times as much per capita as the entire network of EU institutions.

All public debates fall prey to the selective presentation of facts, as well as genuine and unintentional misunderstandings, but the European Union seems to suffer worse than most. It can seem hard to understand, it is a moving target, it seems to threaten the sovereignty of states that many hold so dear, and it is a handy scapegoat for national politicians looking for someone or something else to blame for domestic problems. But no public debate is worth having unless we are at least reasonably clear on the stakes, and in the case of Europe that clarity is often frustratingly remote.

The Confederation of Europe

I have argued, then, that many of the problems in the debate about Europe stem from the difficulty of agreeing precisely what the EU is; in fact it is easier to say what it is not. It is not a standard international organization, for example, because it consists of institutions, networks, obligations and laws that have taken it beyond any other international organization. We also need to remember that 'Europe' is more than the network of EU institutions and agencies; it also includes the political, economic and cultural ties that European states have built with each other outside the meeting rooms of the EU, the regional and local units of government that often have the most direct impact on the lives of Europeans, the millions of

Europeans who have adopted a sense of being European, and the many other European initiatives undertaken by bodies such as the Council of Europe and a broad network of European interest groups and think-tanks.

Neither is the EU a federal European superstate, because to be as much it would need a full-fledged and elected European government with independent powers and responsibilities. None of the two dozen federations in the world (including Germany, Russia, the United States and Canada) look exactly the same, but they all have a distinctive and clearly defined federal government that shares powers with subsidiary state or provincial governments. The EU has some federal qualities, most clearly on show in the work of the European Parliament and the European Central Bank, but the relationship between Bavaria and the German federal government in Berlin is definitely not the same as that between Germany and the European Union institutions in Brussels. We cannot even call the EU a government, because it does not have the same independent powers as national governments to make and enforce law and policy. The best we can say is that it is a process of governance, or an arrangement by which decisions, laws and policies are made without the existence of conventional institutions of government.

What, then, is it? In short, it is a confederation, albeit with some federal qualities. It has never been formally or legally declared as such, and yet it has most of the standard features of a confederation, as a small but impressive club of academics or commentators would attest. As long ago as 1982 the political scientist William Wallace (while admitting that all analogies are inexact) contrasted the European Community with the United States and reflected on the former's confederal qualities.[16] More recently, the Italian scholar Giandomenico Majone suggested that the term *confederation* described 'precisely' the arrangement found in the EU and expressed his regret that confederalism had been 'practically banned from the discourse about the future and finality of the Union'.[17] Not long after that, the Princeton political scientist Andrew Moravcsik argued that the EU was, 'despite a few federal elements, essentially a confederation of member-states',[18] and even *The Economist* has unwittingly agreed, suggesting after the final passage of the Lisbon Treaty in 2009 that 'the union will thus continue as a mainly intergovernmental organization with supranational attributes'.[19] Commission

FEDERATION
Central government

CONFEDERATION
Common authority

States

States

People

People

Federations have two or more levels of government with independent powers and with which the people have a direct political relationship. In confederations, the people relate to a common authority through the states of which they are residents.

Figure 1   Comparing federations and confederations

president José Manuel Barroso threw his hat into the ring during his 2012 State of the Union address when he spoke of the need for the EU 'to move towards a federation of nation states',[20] a term that could easily be construed to mean a confederation.

The confederal features of the EU become clearer when we contrast it with a federation (see Figure 1). The latter is a unified state, within which power is divided between central and local levels of government, and there is a direct link between all levels of government and citizens in the sense that government exercises authority over citizens, and is answerable directly to those citizens. By contrast, a confederation is a group of sovereign states with a central authority deriving its powers from those states, and citizens linked indirectly to the central authority through the states in which they live. As Frederick Lister puts it, if a federation is a union of peoples living within a single state, then a confederation is a union of states.[21]

Unfortunately for those of us who like clear labels, the waters of the debate have been muddied by the federal character of the European Parliament, and by federalizing tendencies in several areas of policy, notably the ever closer ties emerging within the euro zone. The idea of a confederal Europe has also failed to gain much traction in the academic world because of a prevailing fashion to regard the EU as an exercise in multi-level governance, where power is shared among the supranational, national, subnational and local levels of government, with a high degree of interaction.[22] (This is really no more than an elaborate variation on the theme of federalism.) And experience has not been kind to confederations, history telling us that they either fail altogether or evolve into federations. And when Jean Monnet in 1960 outlined a plan for a European confederation, he did so only as a pragmatic step towards an ultimate European federation,[23] helping pave the way for fears among today's eurosceptics that the EU will one day become a European superstate.

But why should the EU not become the world's first sustainable confederation? It is already regarded by most EU scholars as *sui generis*, so why not extend the logic of this argument and acknowledge that it could be the first exception to the curtailed history of confederations? The circumstances behind its creation and development are unparalleled, the trajectory it has followed has been singular, and who is to say that a group of independent states could not move from cooperation to a loose form of political union while still retaining a much greater degree of control over their internal affairs than the standard federation? Given the current balance of opinion about the EU, it would be the compromise most likely to bring together the supporters and opponents of integration.

2   Europe as a Peacemaker

At heart, European integration was always driven by the desire to bring peace to a part of the world once synonymous with war and violence. 'The European Union,' argues former Irish prime minister John Bruton, 'is the world's most successful invention for advancing peace.' For many, the award of the Nobel Peace Prize to the EU in 2012 was well deserved and a fitting recognition of the role that it has played as a peacemaker. So successful has been that role that fear and distrust have been replaced in the region with nonchalance and familiarity, and the idea that European states might go to war with one another again is unthinkable, even laughable. This is a condition that historians call a positive or a sustainable peace.[1]

So normal has peace in Europe become that the novelist Umberto Eco regrets that 'no one realizes how amazing that is any more'.[2] Noting the disappearance of personal memories of war, which he regards as the 'greatest single driving force of the European project since 1945', Timothy Garton Ash concludes that 'the deepest problem of the European project is the problem of success'.[3] Some even suggest that we need a new reason to justify Europe. 'Instead of harping on about the [war],' writes the journalist Gareth Harding, 'pro-Europeans need to develop a new central narrative for the Union that is fit for the 21st century and resonates with a generation whose grandparents were born after 1945.'[4]

But the association between Europe and peace is not just about the end of war. The bigger accomplishment, whose value and relevance continues to grow, has been the creation of a new model for doing political business that emphasizes cooperation over confrontation, diplomacy over war, and civilian power over military power. The EU today is not just at peace with itself, but poses no military threat to others and shows others how they too might achieve a lasting peace. True, it can sometimes appear unwilling or unable to respond to conflicts on its own doorstep, as in Libya or Syria. And true, there is weakness in its need to fall back on the United States in the event of large-scale security threats. And true, it has not entirely eschewed violence as a tool of policy: the larger European states still maintain large militaries and have large defence industries. But unlike any other major global actor, before or since 1945, Europe today is defined in civilian rather than military terms, and it has so abundantly redefined the nature of power and influence that it has left most people struggling to catch up and understand the true significance of its achievement.

Integration cannot be given all the credit for peace in Europe, to be sure. Europeans owe a debt of gratitude to the United States, which paved the way for post-war reconstruction with the Marshall Plan and provided essential security guarantees through the North Atlantic Treaty Organization (NATO). The US has also acted as something of a foil to the self-interested inclinations of many European states, so much so that some have even hinted that a US military withdrawal from Europe might mean a return to military competition among its bigger powers. US leadership not only encouraged western European governments to work together on shared problems after the war, but also gave them the luxury of being able to invest in hospitals and schools rather than guns and warships. The United States also provided policy leadership during the cold war, and while not all Europeans have always agreed with US policy, American presidents have long provided a focus and a sense of direction that is beyond the capacity of a single European leader.

The US has also provided much inadvertent assistance: by pursuing foreign policies that have occasionally alarmed Europeans, it has encouraged them to work together in developing common and distinctive policies of their own. In this respect, Korea, Vietnam, Israel, Iraq and George W. Bush all have their place in the pantheon of European integration: by generating public and political opposition, and showing up European weaknesses, US initiatives pushed Europeans closer together, helping them decide what they had in common, what they believed in, and where their objectives and values have contrasted with those of the United States.

But far less would have been achieved, or so comprehensively, or with such lasting effects, without the cooperative focus provided by European integration. It has encouraged Europeans to work together, to agree shared goals, to open up borders, to bring down trade barriers, and to both deepen and widen the reach of democratic and free market ideas. It has also given them a road map for the peaceful resolution of disputes, and has encouraged them to work together on building economic and social relationships in a manner that has meant the end of the political and military competition that was for so long part of the normal order of European business.

Regional integration has provided Europeans not just with the opportunity and the tools to remove the internal causes of war, but has also forged Europe into an example for the rest of the world. By setting aside the militarism and nationalism that were for so long a defining part of their regional political landscape, Europeans have been able to live out the principle that when states are invested in each other through economic ties, common policies, shared goals, international law, and harmonized standards and regulations, they are less likely to go to war with one another.[5] This has helped European states make longer-term investments in positive peace by mutually reinforcing their democratic and capitalist credentials. This was illustrated first by the boost given by EEC membership to the democratic revival of Greece, Spain and Portugal, and then later by the promotion of the links between peace, democracy and free markets afforded by western European political and economic investment in the post-cold war transition of eastern Europe.

But the European example has global implications, and a review of the different chapters in the story of integration leads us to a critical conclusion: Europe has become the most effective force in history for the spread of sustainable democratic change, and it has done this peacefully, without a single shot being fired. Its achievements were confirmed in 2012, when – in explaining its decision to award the 2012 Nobel Prize for Peace to the European Union – the Nobel committee noted its contributions (and those of its predecessors) over six decades 'to the advancement of peace and reconciliation, democracy and human rights in Europe', recalled its role in making war between France and Germany unthinkable, pointed to its role in encouraging democracy in Greece, Portugal, Spain and post-cold war eastern Europe, and noted the stabilizing role played by the EU in helping 'transform most of Europe from a continent of war to a continent of peace'.

Why Is Europe peaceful?

Until the Second World War, Europe was often a violent and expansionist place. Its leaders regularly took their peoples to war with one another, the conflicts sometimes dragging on for decades. The aggression was later expanded to the global stage through colonial competition and two European civil wars (or three, if we count the Seven Years' War of 1756–63) that became world wars. Military might and the use of force to ring change were defining qualities of the European experience. But since 1945 – and notwithstanding internal conflicts such as those in Northern Ireland and the Balkans, or inter-state disputes such as those between Greece and Turkey or between Britain and Iceland – Europe has been at peace. To what can we credit this remarkable transformation?

The answers are not easy to find, because scholars have spent far more time studying war than they have studying peace. 'For every thousand pages published on the causes of wars,' notes the Australian economic historian Geoffrey Blainey, 'there is less than one page directly on the causes of peace.'[6] Explaining war, argues the American scholar Kenneth Waltz, is easier than understanding the conditions of peace.[7] (This is perhaps why war has been more thoroughly studied. Or is war easier to explain *because* it has been so thoroughly studied?) And even though the pressures that lead to war have been assessed from almost every imaginable angle – including political, economic, philosophical, sociological, psychological and even biological – all that has been agreed is that there is no single cause of war and no single cause of peace.[8] Furthermore, there has been a general decline in the number of wars fought around the world since 1945,[9] so there is a bigger story to tell than the one we find in Europe. There are, in short, many possibilities and few certainties.

John Mearsheimer, a leading American scholar from the realist school of international relations, has few doubts on the matter. Europe has been at peace (at least since 1989), he argues, for two reasons. First, the United States has served as 'Europe's pacifier' or 'night watchman' by maintaining a military presence in the region and keeping NATO intact, thereby ensuring stability. There is little chance that any two NATO states would fight each other, he suggests, because the United States simply 'would not tolerate it',

and the NATO shield also means that European states do not have to worry about threats from Russia and other powers. Second, it has been at peace because most Europeans have welcomed the US presence and accept that the United States has 'a moral and strategic responsibility to run the world'. He gives little credit to the EU for encouraging peace, arguing that talk of the growth of a European identity is not supported by opinion polls, that Europeans have not always been as good at following the rules on integration as they would like to think, and that the EU has failed to produce a meaningful foreign and security policy or an integrated military of its own.[10]

But while there is no question that NATO played a key role in keeping peace in Europe from its creation in 1949 to the end of the cold war, it did so primarily through the threat of violence. It was created in order to send a message to a pugnacious Soviet Union to keep its hands off western Europe, and was based on an agreement that an attack on one member state would be considered an attack on them all. The problem with this rather pessimistic 'peace though strength' philosophy is that it is unlikely to build a positive peace because it is premised on the idea that the world is full of threats and that we need always to be prepared to deal with those threats. Furthermore, NATO has never had the same array of economic incentives and institution-building skills that the EU has been able to bring to bear on a problem.

While the US contribution to European peace was critical in the 1940s and 1950s, the dynamic later changed. Clues to the role of integration can be found in an essay published in 1795 by the German philosopher Immanuel Kant. He was far from being an idealist, and noted that while many empires and great powers had promised that their rule would bring a lasting peace, it had never happened because that rule had been imposed and maintained through violence. The keys to perpetual peace, argued Kant, included the abolition of standing armies, independence and self-determination for individual states, an agreement that no secret treaties would be signed that held out the prospect for future war, and the avoidance by states of acts of hostility during war that would undermine confidence in the peace that followed. The key here was perpetual (or positive) peace, which has been far harder to achieve than temporary (or negative) peace.

It took another 150 years and two world wars before Kant's ideas began to have a wider relevance, and they were reflected in the thoughts of the social scientist David Mitrany, expressed in his 1943 treatise *A Working Peace System*. He argued that the key to peace was 'to weld together the common interests of all without interfering unduly with the particular ways of each', and that the best way of doing this was not through alliances and agreements but by creating functionally specific international agencies with such relatively non-controversial responsibilities as postal services or the harmonization of weights and measures. These agencies would need to coordinate their work across state lines, Mitrany suggested, and success in one area would encourage cooperation in others. Economic and functional ties would lead to political ties, and governments would find themselves linked through a web of international agencies that would leave them less capable of taking independent action. This web of cooperation, he concluded, would result not in a 'protected peace' based on treaties but in a 'working peace'.[11]

For Europeans after 1945, the proximate cause of peace was a simple weariness with war, the lessons of its tragedy and futility being both fresh and abundant. They were also acutely aware of the dangers lurking within punitive peace treaties, needing to look back no further than the 1919 Treaty of Versailles and its role in generating the tensions that led to the Second World War. Hence the priority in 1945 was to rebuild the vanquished rather than to punish them. The cold war provided an additional set of incentives for cooperation: where once Europeans had fretted mainly about each other, they now had to worry about being caught in the crossfire of a conflict involving two much bigger external powers, both armed with large stockpiles of nuclear weapons. To these pressures were added the growing uneasiness in the west with US policy and resentment in the east towards the Soviet hegemony. Europeans had tired of the old balance of power arguments that had so often dragged them into war, and instead sought protection from each other as well as protection from others. Enter European integration, whose contribution to peace has been sixfold.

First, it has neutralized many of the conventional causes of interstate war in the region, such as mistrust, the existence of opposing interests, and the struggle for power and resources. Europeans have become less focused on competing with each other for political influence, the bigger powers no longer see each other as threats, and the effects of improved education and the rise of the middle class have given Europeans similar outlooks and values. Of course they still differ, both among themselves and within their home states and communities, and nationalism has far from disappeared. But where the differences and the competition might once have spilled over into conflict and war, they are now discussed and resolved peaceably and with close attention to the importance of shared and common interests. Europeans are not as easily manipulated as they once were by elites and rabble-rousers seeking to rally people behind national doctrine, and peace has become habit-forming in the sense that Europeans have better understood the benefits of investing in productive rather than destructive activities.

If the lessons of their own history have not been enough, they need only to look at the United States to see the costs that come with maintaining and deploying large militaries. The willingness of the US to take on the burden of security is something for which Europeans can be grateful, even if there is a large measure of self-interest in US policy, but there is a difference between using the military for defensive or offensive purposes. The United States has made several questionable military interventions since 1945 that were defined as being in the national interest, as in Vietnam and Iraq, and in this sense has perpetuated the use of military power where diplomacy might have been more effective. And thanks to the political and economic influence of its enormous defence contractors, and a long history of buying unnecessary or excessively expensive weapons systems,[12] it has spent far more on defence than it needed to, adding dramatically to its budget deficits and national debt, and diverting investments away from education, health care and infrastructure. By contrast, Europeans have come to like their civilian prosperity and wish to see it sustained.

Second, one of the most often suggested causes of war among states is the absence of an authority with the ability to resolve disputes and enforce peace agreements. The EU may not be such an authority, but it has gone one better by building a network of institutions, policies and laws designed to encourage collaboration and investments in the welfare of neighbouring states. Europe no longer has need of old-fashioned dispute resolution because it has adopted the kind of habits of cooperation through shared legal and policy frameworks that prevent serious disputes from emerging and allow disagreements to be resolved peacefully. The result has been the creation of a system of conflict negation, or peace-sustaining habits and procedures that contrast with the widespread readiness of European powers prior to 1939 (or the United States and Russia today) to build and maintain large militaries and to promote self-interest over communal or regional interests.

Where conflicts and wars in other parts of the world continue to demand custom-made diplomacy and peace negotiations, or the commitment of peacekeeping forces, Europeans now have so many networks of consultation in place, and their leaders meet with each other so often in so many different forums, that cooperation is an ongoing phenomenon. Mearsheimer is correct in pointing out that EU states do not always respect or follow their own rules, the mismanagement of the euro being a case in point, but its rule-breaking is not so serious as to create the kind of tensions that would lead to war. European leaders see so much of each other, and meet so often in institutions that have long records of building agreement (even if it has sometimes taken bad-tempered meetings stretching into the small hours of the morning), that any contempt, hostility or doubts they might feel about their peers is more likely to be generated by familiarity than by fear.

Third, integration has encouraged peace by weakening the psychological and political links between Europeans and the states and nations with which they have long identified, and which historically have been the major protagonists in war. Europeans can still take pride in being Hungarian or Dutch or Maltese, but they have set aside notions of superiority over others, and are more ready to look beyond the artificialities of political boundaries to their shared interests, to the compromises they can reach, and to the promotion of big ideas such as democracy, peace, human rights and free markets. Where once they might have seen their neighbours as threats, or at least as exotic foreigners, they are now more likely to see them as partners who look, dress, talk and generally act much like themselves. As we will see in Chapter 5, many Europeans now view malignant nationalism and state-based patriotism with suspicion, and there is a growing sense of identification with Europe, which represents engagement in a common project and an absence of the kinds of pressures that have so often led in the past to war and conflict. As the financier George Soros puts it, the EU is 'the embodiment of an

---

Box 2: Seven reasons why Europe is peaceful

1. The United States has provided a security umbrella and economic leadership.
2. The integration of Europe has neutralized many of the conventional causes of inter-state war.
3. The EU has created a network of collaborative institutions that offset the pressures that might lead to conflict.
4. Europeans identify more with inclusive ideas such as democracy, peace and human rights, and less with patriotism and malignant nationalism.
5. Free trade and the opening of European markets has removed many of the traditional causes of conflict.
6. Democracy and integration have created a perpetual cycle of peace.
7. Europe defines itself less in military than in social terms, has diverted investments from military to civilian ends, and has replaced preparations for war with a focus on social investment.

---

open society – an association of nations founded on the principles of democracy, human rights, and rule of law in which no nation or nationality would have a dominant position'.[13]

Fourth, capitalist peace theory tells us that an international market economy driven by free trade is the best guarantor of peace, and that restrictions on trade (such as tariffs and quotas) may cause tensions that might lead to war. In other words, because people or countries that trade with one another will have a vested interest in each other's wealth and welfare, they will be more inclined to work peacefully with each other to solve problems, resolve disputes and open markets. Consider the arguments made by the economist Joseph Schumpeter: capitalism, he said, produces a population that is 'democratized, individualized, [and] rationalized', whose energy is focused on production, that demands democracy, and that is more interested in having a government that promotes peace than one retaining an interest in war. When free trade prevails, he argued, raw materials become more easily available and all can share in the benefits they provide.[14] Open markets also have the benefit of taking many economic decisions out of the hands of states, removing many of the suspicions that can lead to tensions.[15]

Fifth, democracies rarely if ever go to war with each other. There have been several explanations for what is known among scholars as democratic peace theory: leaders of democracies must answer to their electorates and thus have more incentive to peacefully resolve problems (or at the very least to factor public opinion into decisions to go to war); democratic governments are more used to settling disputes through negotiation; and wealthy or powerful states tend to avoid war because they have more to lose. The United States, still under the thrall of the military–industrial complex, is one exception to this rule, but even there politicians must be careful to keep public opinion on their side. There is something to be learned from the (albeit not entirely accurate) proposition that no two countries that have McDonalds outlets within their borders have gone to war with one another.[16]

Democratic peace theory has its critics, many of whom charge that the element of 'peace' is often tenuous at best, but it was Kant's belief that a positive peace could be developed within a federation of sovereign states resting on democracy, interdependence, and international law and organizations, and that the absence of these conditions would result in the prospect of violence remaining.[17] Europe has put Kantian ideas into practice, but Europeans have gone further: they not only avoid going to war with one another, but they generally prefer not to go to war with anyone else, and have expanded the prospects for peace to their neighbourhood. To those, then, who would argue that the Second World War ended a long time ago and we need a new reason to justify Europe, we need look only at the lasting effects on peace of the European project and the example that the achievement and maintenance of peace in Europe offers to others.

Finally, peace in Europe can be explained simply by a change in attitude. Before the First World War, suggests the historian Michael Howard, 'war was almost universally considered an acceptable, perhaps and inevitable and for many people a desirable way of settling international differences'.[18] The expanded reach of international cooperation and law has made war less publically acceptable, and the glorification of war has declined markedly. Europeans now give much less weight to the military in their definition of national identities and foreign policy goals, and focus instead on social invest-ment. For centuries, there was an intimate link in Europe between military power, the definition of national interests, the priorities of economic development, and inter-state relations; we have only to consider the battlefields, war graves, memorials and statues of dead generals that litter the European landscape. But it is impossible now to look at these reminders of past conflicts without appreciating just how thoroughly Europeans have rejected the notion of war. The fiscal-military state of the past, which relied on large armed forces supported by funding through unprecedented levels of taxation and government borrowing,[19] is gone. Swords have not entirely been turned into ploughshares, and Europe still has large militaries, large military budgets, and profitable weapons manufacturers, but Europeans have eschewed the warfare state in favour of the welfare state, and are less interested in war and preparation for war than in peace and the distribution of the dividends of peace.

It is possible that Europe would have achieved a lasting peace with-out the creation of European institutions and the habits of cooperation and integration that followed in their wake. The cold war, for exam-ple, encouraged a nervous form of peace – in the sense that name-call-ing was preferable to nuclear annihilation. And American policy hawks might have argued that a post-cold war world safeguarded by a US military hegemony would have guaranteed global peace. But history has shown that the existence of great powers routinely results in other powers organizing themselves as a counterbalance, and that a positive peace cannot be guaranteed through the threat of violence. As Albert Einstein put it, one cannot simultaneously prevent and prepare for war. This was something that Kant understood, and that is today understood and embraced by most Europeans.

Civilian Power Europe

In a world of uncertainty and danger, many of us continue to be reas-sured and impressed by large militaries, and no one impresses us more than the United States. It has large corporations, the strongest currency in the world, and a culture that even its sharpest critics find seductive, but when it comes to making a point about raw and uncompromising power, nothing beats the sight of smart bombs raining down on Baghdad or US aircraft carriers cruising majestically through the Strait of Hormuz.

Military power remains central to security, to be sure, and large militaries can be highly effective at offering a deterrent or in responding to an attack. The United States has the biggest and most technologically advanced military in the world, spread across more than 700 military bases worldwide as well as nearly 4900 within the United States and its territories,[20] and supported by an annual budget that accounts for nearly half of global military spending.[21] Small wonder, then, that when a new threat looms, it is to the White House or the State Department or the Pentagon that the eyes and the television cameras of much of the world turn.

But there is disconcertingly little evidence that military power has the capacity to bring permanent and positive change. For every example of success (the defeat and democratic transformation of Germany and Japan being the obvious standouts) there are multiple examples of failure and doubt (including Afghanistan, Grenada, Haiti, Lebanon, Nicaragua, Panama, Somalia and Thailand).[22] Hard power and violence might bring a short-term peace, but it can also drag its protagonists into lengthy and expensive military commitments, and forcing change at the end of a barrel of a gun usually results in resentful acquiescence rather than a willing conversion.

The nature of warfare is also changing, both in terms of its participants and its methods. A study by Canadian researchers of conflicts between 1945 and 2008 found that wars were mainly fought within rather than between states and that they had become less deadly in terms of the number of casualties[23]; thus civil war is a greater danger than inter-state war, raising demands entirely different policy decisions. Conflict has become more a matter of helping states sort out their internal problems than preparing for threats or invasions from those states. Also, suggests American political scientist Anne-Marie Slaughter, the era of large-scale multi-year conflicts involving ground invasions of one country by another is probably over, and, at least among the major powers, conflict is more likely to be fought on the digital frontier, conducted by special forces, and targeted at individuals rather than states or large groups.[24]

Make no mistake: the EU is a substantial military actor, at least if we add up the personnel, hardware, firepower and military budgets of the member states. In 2010–11, they spent about $230 billion on defence, and while this was less than half the US total, it was more than China, Russia, India and Japan combined. Together they have more active personnel (about 1.7 million) than the United States, and bigger navies and air forces than China and India combined.[25] And the common perception that the EU shies away from military engagement does not gel with the facts: personnel from EU member states have been involved in almost all the major conflicts of recent decades, from the Balkans to Iraq, Afghanistan, Libya and (if we add bilateral activities by Britain and France) Sierra Leone, Côte d'Ivoire, and Mali. And in the face of cuts to defence budgets, EU states have been working to avoid duplication in functions and planning their spending so as to be stronger while also achieving economies of scale.

But Europeans do not much like war, whether at home or abroad, and would rather that their militaries be used for peacekeeping than for peacemaking. The long-term effect is that integration has helped mould the EU into a new kind of actor on the global stage, which eschews military power in favour of using economic, diplomatic and cultural instruments to achieve objectives, and which prefers international cooperation, the use of persuasion, and democratic civilian control over foreign and defence policymaking.[26] In short, Europeans – shaped by decades of peaceful cooperation – prefer to achieve their goals by hosting meetings rather than launching missiles.

Where Europeans once lauded their military and regarded it as essential both to national identity and to the defence of national interests (much as the US continues to do today), European states have become classic examples of what the sociologist Martin Shaw describes as post-military societies: they have ceased to allow the military and militarism to dominate political calculations and social relations, and have instead become pacifist while maintaining small and professional armed forces.[27] A combination of revulsion at their historical excesses and a belief in the peaceful and collective resolution of tensions has given European states – encouraged by their work within the EU – a distinctive personality driven by three principles:

- *Civilian power*, or a preference for non-military and mainly economic means to achieving their goals, leaving the military as a residual safeguard, and preferring cooperation to conflict.[28]
- *Soft power*, or a preference for shaping rather than forcing the positions of others, co-opting rather than coercing, using

influence rather than threats, and encouraging others to want the same outcomes.[29]

- *Multilateralism*, or a belief that states should work together rather than heading off in isolation, and that emphasizes rules, cooperation, inclusiveness, and the building of a sustainable consensus.[30]

Where war, and preparation for war, was once central to the definition of European power, this is no longer the case. In his book *Where Have All the Soldiers Gone?*, the historian James Sheehan argues that European states once glamourized their military elites, made war the highest expression of patriotism, and celebrated military achievements in their civic culture. We still find variations on these themes in the United States, where Americans – argues historian Andrew Bacevich – are 'seduced' by war and believe in 'a marriage of militarism and utopian ideology; of unprecedented military might wed to a blind faith in the universality of American values'.[31] By contrast, Europeans mainly prefer to avoid violence as a tool of statecraft, have reimagined the meaning of statehood, and have rejected expanding defence budgets in favour of material well-being, social stability and economic growth.

Sheehan goes on to note the rise of a European 'civilian state', its roots found in the rapid economic growth of western Europe during

---

Box 3: Seven advantages of civilian power

1. It creates fewer threats, suspicions or tensions than military power.
2. It is more likely than military power to bring durable democratic change.
3. It is less costly in human and financial terms than military power.
4. It focuses on economic means to achieve national goals.
5. It is based on co-option rather than on coercion, and on peace rather than violence.
6. It allows resources to be diverted to peaceful means.
7. It has more relevance and utility to the solution of problems such as poverty.

the 1950s by virtue of which the legitimacy of every western European government came to depend on its capacity to sustain growth and prosperity, and to provide generous social services.[32] If cold war US policy was driven by the need to remain secure in the face of the Soviet threat, cold war western European policy was driven by the need to grow economies and welfare systems.

It was in the 1960s, in the depths of the cold war and against the background of Vietnam, that speculation began to emerge of Europe's potential to be a different kind of global power based on what the British journalist Anthony Sampson described as 'new kinds of society, new political ideas, [and] new philosophies'.[33] The concept of civilian power was introduced by François Duchêne (biographer of Jean Monnet), who suggested that a lack of military power was no longer the handicap that it had once been, and speculated that western Europe might become the world's first civilian centre of power. This he defined as one 'where the age-old process of war and indirect violence could be translated into something more in tune with the twentieth-century citizen's notion of civilized politics'.[34]

As Europe integrated, Duchêne argued, there was little purpose in it trying to build a European army because there was now more scope for civilian forms of action and influence. Indeed, Europe's lack of military power could actually be an advantage because it removed suspicions about European intentions and allowed it to act as an unbiased moderator. In short, he concluded, Europe offered the prospect of a new definition of great power based on civilian forms of influence and action.[35] This may all sound irredeemably idealistic to those who would argue that military power is essential to security, and that it is the only commodity understood by Somali warlords, North Korean dictators or Afghan religious zealots. And what about those security problems that keep bubbling up on the borders of Europe? How can it be an effective crisis manager without a security and defence policy or an integrated military? Consider, however, the many disadvantages of military power.

To begin with, it does not always prevail, as reflected in the many historical examples of Goliaths being stopped in their tracks by Davids: the French in Algeria, the Americans in Vietnam, the Soviets in Afghanistan, and – more recently – the unconvincing outcome of the wars in Iraq and Afghanistan. Even today there is a myth abroad that the president of the United States is the most powerful person in the world (the leader of the 'free world') and that he has the resources at his disposal to bend history to his will. Nothing could be further from the truth, argues Andrew Bacevich; presidents are constrained by 'forces that lie beyond their grasp and perhaps their understanding' and are 'much more likely to dance to history's tune'.[36] And what of the claim by former US Secretary of State Madeleine Albright that the US is the 'indispensable nation' that stands tall and sees 'further into the future'?[37] This all depends on what we mean by indispensable, and how we interpret what we see in that future.

Militaries are also expensive in both human and financial terms, diverting resources away from other endeavours that are often better investments in the security and happiness of societies. Americans would probably be more content, more secure and more fulfilled if they followed the European lead and spent more of their tax dollars on schools, hospitals and infrastructure than on weapons systems that the military often neither wants nor needs. Thanks mainly to habits cultivated through the EU, Europe is at peace, it threatens no one, and it faces few threats that cannot be addressed more effectively by careful diplomacy (such as unfinished business in the Balkans, or new belligerence from Russia), or (like the threat of international terrorism) can only partly be addressed by the maintenance of militaries. The resulting savings have been diverted into investments in society, a position that leaves Europeans not just peaceful but relatively content and generally better served by facilities and infrastructure than their well-armed American peers.

Large militaries can also create tensions where none might otherwise have existed, perhaps encouraging weaker states to build militaries to protect themselves from stronger states. Consider here the worries that have been generated by the recent growth of China's defence spending. Consider also the belligerent posture of small states such as North Korea, Iran and Venezuela; at least part of their aggression can be explained by their feeling cornered and threatened by the massive military power of the United States. The best response to them is not more aggression but rather the kind of diplomacy and incentives preferred by the EU. As Winston Churchill once pointed out, 'to jaw-jaw' is always better than 'to war-war'. And as if this is not enough, militaries are all but irrelevant when it comes to dealing with many of the most pressing problems we face today, such as climate change, poverty and disease.

Critics have a point when they argue that Europeans can only afford the luxury of a civilian economy so long as the United States is there to provide insurance by stepping into the breach when needed. The achievement of peace in Europe after 'ages of ruinous warfare' was a great achievement, argued US Defense Secretary Robert Gates in 2010, but the trend had 'gone too far' with the failure by European governments to invest in weapons and equipment. This, he concluded, might lead to a perception of weakness among hostile states.[38] Perhaps, but it might also be interpreted as the signal achievement of European integration: without large militaries and defence budgets, Europe poses less of a threat to itself and to others, creates fewer tensions, and is able to invest more in social and economic development.

Let us again speculate about what might have happened in a Europe without the European Union. It is entirely possible that the groundswell of support for peace that followed the Second World War would have been translated into a peaceful Europe where governments and people worked out different means for living in tranquillity and removing the mechanisms and stresses that for hundreds of years had led them down the path to conflict and war. But even though the kinds of pressures that took Europe from the First World War to the Second World War were almost entirely missing from the landscape after 1945, it is unlikely that peace would have been so positive without the removal of the pressures, proclivities and perspectives that had for so long made Europeans so ready to go to war with one another.

The region faced an entirely new set of circumstances after the war, not least being caught – for the first time in its history – in the tensions between two much greater external powers, the United States and the Soviet Union. But while the cold war brought a disturbed form of peace to the region, it could never be assured or permanent without the creation of the webs of cooperation and reciprocity that were made possible by the European project. Peace might have been achieved, but it would not have been because Europeans had worked together to make it happen. More importantly, Europe would not have been able to become the force for the spread of democracy and free markets – and the deserving winner of a Nobel Prize for Peace – quite so quickly or convincingly as it has.

3 Europe as a Marketplace

Ask Europeans what the European project means to them, and most will quickly point to the single market and the euro. Even if much else about the EU puzzles them, most can readily relate to the single market, the one part of the European project that has most clearly changed their lives and that has the widest support. The euro, meanwhile, was intended to be the glue that held the single market together, clearing the path to the final achievement of Europe's famous 'four freedoms': the unrestricted movement of people, money, goods and services. There has been a great deal to celebrate in the single market, and the benefits of a single currency will become clear again once the problems of the euro have been resolved. But both initiatives have suffered from a distinct lack of political courage: too many barriers remain to the single market, and not enough has been done to provide the euro with the features it needs to be a real success.

In the credit column of the ledger, the single market has greatly improved life for Europeans. It has generated new jobs (or, at least, new jobs in different areas), offered consumers a greater variety of goods and services at lower prices, promoted competition that has led to improved service and new products, created a new hinterland for European business, reduced the number of technical standards and regulations, eliminated discriminatory taxes on goods and services, introduced stronger and uniform protection for consumers, provided a cleaner environment for Europeans, improved personal safety in the wake of better police and judicial cooperation, and opened access to a broader and deeper pool of ideas and talent as Europeans work together to seek the solution to economic and social problems. It has done all this on the back of a distinctive model of economic growth that is both kinder and greener than before, and more focused on quality over quantity.

Many of the benefits have been serendipitous. Consider, for example, the progress on environmental cooperation, an idea that

47

did not even remotely occur to the framers of the Treaty of Rome. Pressures to remove barriers to the single market have since resulted in a more efficient and effective approach to the reduction of air and water pollution, the management of chemicals, the production and disposal of waste, the generation and use of renewable energy, and the improved protection of wildlife and natural habitats. Consider also the efforts to protect and harmonize the interests of consumers, guarding them against price gouging and mixed safety standards. There was barely a hint of this in Rome, but clearly there could be no meaningful open market unless consumers had such rights.

The single market has also encouraged the rise of global European corporations, which has meant new investments in research and development, job creation, the development of new products and services, new tax revenues, meeting competition from abroad, and expanding the global economic influence of the EU. (This is discussed in more depth in Chapter 7.) There has also been rapid progress since the mid-1990s with cooperation on cross-border crime, helping police forces and courts to work together in their pursuit of lawbreakers who might otherwise have been hard to reach. And the EU has helped channel enormous investments into the building of cross-border highways and railways, opening up new and improved connections within the European marketplace.

Even Europe's once controversial agricultural policy has not been all bad. Yes, it has been interventionist and expensive, leading to market distortions, waste and over-production as well as swallowing up much of the EU budget. But it has also helped boost the productivity of Europe's farmers, contributed to improved food safety and quality, promoted improved animal health and welfare, encouraged innovation in farming techniques and food processing, and poured enormous investment into previously marginalized rural areas. Trade policy has also been a success, blending the power of the member states into the world's biggest trading bloc, with all the economic advantages this has meant. And competition policy has been effective at helping guard against the building of monopolies and the abuse by corporations of their dominant market positions, further protecting the interests of consumers and offering them more goods and services at lower prices.

But the debit column in the single market ledger remains too crowded. The biggest problem is that too many barriers remain, and not enough has been done to open up opportunities, encourage competition, promote social mobility, and reduce economic inequality. There are still limits on the movement of people (particularly from east to west), tax rates vary, unemployment is too high, the EU has lagged in the promotion of e-commerce, the financial services and banking markets are not yet fully open, multiple standards and regulations often still apply to goods produced in different countries, and language differences remain a potent barrier to the free flow of workers. There have been well-meaning efforts to respond, such as the launch in 2000 of the Lisbon Strategy to make the EU the most dynamic and competitive knowledge-based economy in the world within ten years (a deadline later extended to 2020). But there is too much complacency, with Europe's leaders often unwilling to take (or even sometimes fully to understand) the steps needed to make economic integration more efficient, and to take care of unfinished business.

Meanwhile, defining the natural boundaries of the single market remains difficult. Efforts to bring down borders have led to policy spillover that has pushed the EU into areas never anticipated by the Treaty of Rome, including environmental protection, research and development, immigration and asylum, consumer rights, education, energy, and labour mobility. While there is often a clear logic to this process, and unanticipated benefits, it has also sparked much of the reaction against integration: every step to expand the policy reach of the EU is seen by critics as another retreat for the independence and sovereignty of the member states. In this respect, few initiatives have been more controversial than the euro. The retention of national currencies would have meant the persistence of roadblocks within the European marketplace, including transaction costs, losses created by changes in exchange rates, and the psychological reminders to European travellers of their differences. Thus exchange rate stability was part of the European project from the beginning, and the single currency was long seen as the essential final step in completing the single market.

But all did not work out as intended. The euro lacked a mechanism for centralized control over borrowing and spending; then Greece was allowed to join even though it had not met all the stability criteria for entry; and several euro zone states (including Germany and France) broke their own rules on budget deficits. The global financial crisis shed light on Greece's fiscal misdeeds, the euro zone crisis broke, and matters were made worse by political dithering and a lack of decisive action on the part of Germany and France. But it is worth remembering that even as the crisis unfolded, the euro retained the support of large majorities in every euro zone state (although enthusiasm inevitably wavered as the euro's problems deepened), and the core advantages of a well-designed and managed single currency remain mainly uncontested: convenience, savings, transparency, the psychological benefits of a shared currency, and the international political reach that comes from controlling one of the world's major currencies.

The Single Market

The single market is the crown jewel of European integration, lying at the heart of the efforts by European states to cooperate and integrate. Even most eurosceptics will acknowledge its merits, arguing that the European project should always have been about free trade, rather than about straying into other areas of policy. The problem, of course, is that it was always impossible to draw clear lines of demarcation around the single market; the efforts to achieve the four freedoms repeatedly revealed new barriers and handicaps that had not occurred to the framers of the Treaty of Rome, obliging the EU member states to pool more control over new areas of policy.

Spillover might be interpreted as an insidious phenomenon by which political ambition and the invisible hand of the marketplace have pushed Europeans into new areas of cooperation, eating into the sovereignty of member states while expanding the body of EU law and the authority of the EU institutions. But it can also be interpreted as a benign, essential and sensible process by which the benefits of integration have been broadened and its procedures made more efficient, tying up loose ends, removing unhelpful bottlenecks, and creating new and logical opportunities. Spillover is also a natural ingredient in the process of responding to changes in the dynamics of the marketplace; how, after all, could the framers of Rome have predicted the rise of globalization and the digital marketplace?

Polls reveal that Europeans agree on the benefits of a single market by the convincing margin of more than two to one. Even in the doldrums of the euro zone crisis in the summer of 2011, 67 per cent of respondents in a 13-state opinion poll believed that EU membership had been good for their national economies.[1] The benefits of the single market show themselves in ways that are relatively easy to see and experience:

- The days of long queues at border crossings and of sometimes onerous customs and immigration requirements are almost entirely gone. With some limits, citizens of one member state can live, work, start a business, buy a home, get an education or retire in any other member state. In many cases, the only remaining physical indication of borders that might once have been guarded by tanks and bunkers are signs announcing that a traveller is about to enter a new country.

- Bringing down frontier controls has meant new prosperity and opportunity. The single market has contributed to the growth of GDP and new jobs (although just how much is impossible to say with any certainty). It has also provided new incentives for interstate trade, and for the creation and expansion of businesses. To be sure, there have been job losses as competition has grown and the market has adjusted, but this is a normal part of the cycle of economic change, and to blame the EU for such losses is too simple. That there is still high long-term unemployment in many parts of the EU, for example, is at least in part the result of too little integration (remaining handicaps to the labour market) rather than too much.

- The opening of markets, the breaking down of monopolies, the discouragement of protectionism and the growth of competition has meant the offering of a wider selection of goods and services to European consumers at lower prices, as well as improvements in quality and a tightening of safety standards.

- The harmonization of laws has meant a reduction in the number and complexity of national standards and regulations and their replacement with Europe-wide systems, decreasing the bureaucratic burdens on business, removing the need for expensive and sometimes time-consuming testing in multiple countries, and cutting delivery times and costs. Complaints that there has been over-regulation in some parts of the single market are not without justification, it must be said, and explain the current commitment of the European Commission to regulate less and better.

- European business has been given access to a far bigger market, allowing it to play to its strengths, employ economies of scale, make greater profits, create new jobs, and compete more effectively with non-European corporations.
- A host of European Court of Justice decisions have helped even the playing field and remove discriminatory laws: nationals of one member state can set up a business in another member state on the same basis as locals, pregnant women cannot be fired from their jobs, students who want to study in another member state cannot be charged higher fees, national football federations cannot limit the number of foreign players on domestic teams, and EU nationals can obtain medical treatment in another member state and be reimbursed at the same rates they would receive at home.

As well as the many focused changes it has wrought, the single market has had four broader effects. First, and as we saw in Chapter 2, the economic ties that Europeans have woven among themselves have resulted in their being so heavily invested in each other's welfare that the stresses and pressures that once might have led to conflict and war are mainly gone. Corporate and economic ties have given EU states a deep vested interest in their mutual welfare; what happens in one has come to matter a great deal to the others, and where once they might have been tempted to protect national champions and national markets, setting up barriers to trade and in the worst cases engaging in the rattling of sabres, they are now more likely to air their grievances in the climate-controlled comfort of a meeting room in Brussels.

The single market has also had the important psychological effect of making the foreign more accessible and familiar. Economies and markets were once defined on national lines, and cross-border travel was once an epic adventure that left people negotiating customs and immigration, shopping in unfamiliar stores for unfamiliar products subject to different standards and regulations, and having to learn different ways of doing business. The cultural differences remain, and long may that continue to be so, but integration has removed most of the minor irritants of travel, allowing consumers and business to cross borders so actively and routinely as to allow Europeans to become familiar with different environments and see the same products and corporate logos on display, as well as buying the same services operating on the same rules. They can also continue to buy uniquely local products, confident in the knowledge that they are subject to the same health and safety controls.

Second, the single market has provided an expanded local base for European trade. More than 70 per cent of exports from EU member states go to other EU member states, by far the largest proportion for any group of contiguous countries in the world. This has provided EU businesses with a massive new hinterland, helping them offset competition from outsiders. As illustration of the costs of a failure to promote internal trade, we need only look at Latin America, where even emerging powers such as Brazil have found themselves losing ground to outsiders entering their markets. The problem has been the slowness with which neighbouring Latin American states – anxious to protect burgeoning industrial sectors – have removed mutual barriers to trade.[2] Rather than reverting to protectionism, these states would be better advised to follow the European lead by bringing down barriers and expanding opportunities for local businesses.

Third, the binding of the European marketplace – and the expansion of the opportunities thus made available – has provided new funds and incentives for the building of infrastructure and networks designed to better connect the parts to the whole. Consider, for example, the trans-European networks (TENs) programme aimed at integrating transport, energy supply and telecommunications systems across the EU, and removing variations in the quality and reach of transport networks that put some parts of the EU at an economic disadvantage while creating more congestion in others. The programme has helped link major cities, better connecting wealthier and poorer parts of the EU, helping revitalize rail transport, supporting high-speed rail systems, expanding the 'motorways of the sea' (shipping lanes around the coasts of the EU), improving the ability of producers to convey their goods to market, creating new jobs and market opportunities, and contributing to the reduction of oil dependency and greenhouse emissions.

But while much has been achieved on the transport front, much remains to be done. On the one hand, EU law has helped liberalize air transport, allowed trucks to operate in multiple countries (helping remove the need for them to return empty on international trips, and making better use of time and energy), opened up much of the long-range rail freight system to competition, and encouraged the greening of transport. Ordinary Europeans see the changes most clearly in the rise of transport options, the better links between rail, road and air networks across Europe, and the improvement of rail and road links. On the other hand, the connections among national transport networks are still often incomplete. Railways, for example, are disjointed as a result of different track gauges and signalling systems, rules protecting favoured operators, and variable track quality, and the single market does not extend to the sea, where ships are subject to full customs formalities when they sail from one EU port to another.[3] The Single European Sky project has also made little progress since its launch in 2002. It has the noble goal of creating a single European airspace that would triple capacity, improve safety, cut air traffic management costs in half, modernize sometimes archaic technology, and reduce the environmental impact of flying, but fragmentation along national lines persists.

Finally, there is the effect of the single market on the place of Europe in the international system. The global economy is an often stormy sea upon whose surface small countries and corporations can find themselves tossed with an alarming loss of control. Competition will only tighten as the global rise of China and India continues, and it is delusional to believe that even Europe's major economies can go it alone, or that they are better placed to compete without the smoothing effect of EU regulations. The EU's smaller economies face even greater threats, as the shocks of the global financial crisis revealed in the contrasting cases of Iceland and Ireland. As part of the EU, the latter had access to more immediate financial help than the former, whose previously lukewarm position on EU membership quickly changed; Iceland lodged its application for EU membership in 2009. Meanwhile, there may be much nostalgic attraction in Scotland to the idea of independence, but the financial crisis made it clear to Scots how useful it was to have the British government available to bail out its two biggest banks, RBS and HBOS.[4]

Consumers have been among the primary beneficiaries of single market law, which has both broadened their options and given them new levels of protection. Thanks to the opening up of the airline

Box 4: Twelve benefits of the single European market

1. Open borders with near complete freedom of movement.
2. Bigger markets, creating new jobs and increasing profits.
3. Creation of webs of economic interest that minimize pressures for conflict and war.
4. Reduced protectionism, more competition and improved economies of scale.
5. A greater variety of goods and services available at lower prices.
6. New efforts to integrate transport, energy supply and telecommunications systems.
7. EU economies able to work together to weather international competition.
8. Improved consumer protection and workplace safety standards.
9. Improved environmental quality.
10. Educational choices for students in multiple countries, and transferability of degrees.
11. The growth of European multinational corporations encouraged.
12. More options for the EU for soft political and economic influence.

market, where governments once fiercely protected their so-called national carriers (even if they made large losses), the number of airlines has grown, airlines have been allowed to operate on more routes, there has been a growth in the number of cut-price airlines, and ticket prices have fallen: the days when it was sometimes cheaper to fly from one European city to another via the United States than directly are long gone. Passenger rights have also been strengthened, starting with air passengers, expanding later to train and ship passengers, and ending with laws directed at travel on buses and coaches. They include the right to information on delays, compensation in the event of overbooking, cancellation or delays, the end of hidden charges in ticket prices, and special attention for passengers with disabilities. Common standards have also been set for air transport security, including rules on the screening of passengers and baggage, and on staff recruitment and training.

Consider other single market laws with benefits for consumers:

- With the break-up of telephone monopolies, the creation of new service providers and regulations on charges, the costs of using phones has been falling steadily across the EU since the late 1990s. Additionally, EU law will in 2014 put an end to the practice by service providers of raising roaming costs for consumers outside their home states. As well as placing a cap on the cost of calls, texting and data transfer, the law also allows consumers to choose a different operator abroad than the one they use at home. The Commission has also persuaded mobile phone makers (without the passage of new laws) to replace multiple mobile phone chargers with a single micro-USB plug, reducing costs and inconvenience to customers and reducing electrical waste.

- Consumers were once subject to higher charges when they used credit or debit cards outside their home countries, or withdrew cash from ATMs. EU law since 2002 has imposed a standard charge regardless of country, and since 2003 there has been a standard charge for transfers from one bank account to another.

- A law passed in 1998 made it easier for anyone involved in a road accident in another member state to make insurance claims in their home state.

- There has been a prohibition on unfair, misleading, aggressive or coercive approaches to selling products and services, particularly to children.

While critics charge that EU law has strayed too far into areas of national policy, others – particularly business and consumer groups – argue that it has not gone far enough. For example, while much has been done to liberalize trade in goods, progress on the liberalization of trade in services has been more modest. While changes on the merchandise front mean that almost half of global trade in goods now involves Europe in some fashion, there are substantial unmet possibilities on the services front. Services account for 75 per cent of the GDP of the EU and for about 70 per cent of jobs, and yet cross-border services account for only five per cent of the GDP of the EU compared to the 17 per cent contributed by trade in goods.[5] A Services Directive was adopted in 2006 that was intended to address many of the obstacles, but numerous hurdles remain: the buyers and sellers of financial services and products are often prevented from dealing with one another across borders by different national rules on everything from investor protection to information disclosure, insider trading, takeovers and pension provision.

The benefits of a single market in financial services would include lower transaction costs, the ability to invest and raise funds in every member state, cross-border competition, more opportunities to pool risk, less duplication and inefficiency, more choice for consumers, economies of scale, and the ability to allocate savings and investments to their most productive uses.[6] EU law has provided standard guarantees for bank depositors in every EU state, and since 2001 has allowed homebuyers – once limited to taking out mortgages in their home country – to shop across borders and compare costs, while mortgage lenders have been required to publish detailed information on the services they provide. Efforts to clean up in the wake of the euro zone crisis have led to key changes in the financial services sector, with better supervision, improved early warning systems, and new approaches to insider trading, market abuse and caps on bonuses. But more needs to be done.

The EU has also made too little progress in its efforts to create a digital single market, where it lags far behind the United States. Given the rapid growth in the number of consumers and companies using the internet to do business, the continued fragmentation of the European digital market not only slows down economic growth but works particularly against smaller companies that are heavy users of technology. Consumers are discouraged from using the internet for cross-border purchases because of concerns about speed, cost, safety of delivery and security of payments. Furthermore, the EU does not yet train enough communication technology professionals, high-speed broadband access remains limited, and companies must deal with different contract law and tax systems.[7] By one estimate, a digital single market could add four per cent to the GDP of the EU within ten years, offering consumers more choice at lower process, and promoting growth and innovation.[8] So once again the issue is not that integration has gone too far, but that it has not gone far enough, and that policymakers need to catch up with the opportunities to be had from removing barriers and handicaps. Consumers are leading the way as they become more conscious of prices and more active seekers of the bargains often available online. But while online purchases are growing within EU member states, cross-border trade remains marginal.

Another area in which there has been too little progress has been in encouraging new business start-ups, particularly in the areas of IT and biotechnology. While changes to the law and the business environment have helped pave the way for large new European multinationals that are competing head to head with their American rivals (see Chapter 7), there has been what *The Economist* describes as a 'chronic failure to encourage ambitious entrepreneurs' in the EU. Big companies tend not to like dealing with small ones, entrepreneurs often leave the stultified air of Europe for more open pastures in the United States, bankruptcies can take years to discharge (contributing to a culture of risk aversion), and venture capital is often hard to attract.[9] The result is that while the United States produces new and innovative companies like Apple, Google and Amazon, the EU does not; while the US gave birth to 51 new big companies in the period 1950–2000, and emerging markets gave birth to 46, Europe gave birth to just 12.[10] 'We stifle innovation,' laments former Spanish prime minister Felipe Gonzalez. 'This is why Europe has failed to produce a Bill Gates.'[11]

The EU has not forgotten the interests of smaller companies, known as small and medium enterprises (SMEs). Defined as independent companies with fewer than 250 employees (although most have fewer than ten) and an annual turnover of less than €50 million, they account for two-thirds of private sector jobs, have a critical role in the EU's economic growth, and have been prominent on the agenda of European economic policy. For example, the 2008 Small Business Act for Europe is designed to make it easier for people to start their own businesses, and to access contracts, loans and research funding. EU law on late payments has also been a particular boon to SMEs; when someone provides a service and the client is late paying the fee, the cost is passed on to the provider, a problem that interferes with the functioning of the single market, distorts competition, and can be a crippling burden to small companies. A 2011 EU directive reduces late payments by setting common standards and requirements for all the member states. The EU is also working on a programme to make it easier for entrepreneurs to access venture capital across borders.

The benefits of the single market have not been restricted to the economic sector, but have been felt in other policy areas as well. Prime among those has been the environment, where different standards would interfere with the single market by allowing member states with higher standards to block imports from those with lower standards, and would tempt companies wanting to avoid the cost burden of higher standards to close factories and move them to countries with lower standards. An integrated European approach to environmental management has resulted in laws and policies that have made Europe cleaner, safer, and even quieter (there is a substantial body of laws on noise pollution). They have also helped the EU become a global leader, because any foreign companies or countries hoping to do business in the EU are expected to meet European environmental standards. And Europeans appreciate the benefits: Eurobarometer polls show that more than two-thirds believe that decisions on the environment are better taken jointly at the EU level than at the national level.[12] But again there is room for improvement, one study suggesting that improved energy efficiency alone could create two million new jobs, result in savings in energy production of €8–17 billion per year by 2020, save consumers up to €1000 in energy costs per household, and – through reductions in greenhouse gases – generate health benefits worth €60–80 billion.[13]

Speculating on how matters might have unfolded without the European Union is not easy. Market pressures would have led to some of the changes brought by the single market, but the example of other parts of the world with close economic and trading ties suggests that such changes would have taken longer to achieve or would not have gone so far. Free trade has long been an idea to which governments have paid lip service, but the temptation to protect national companies and markets has strong appeals for voters, business and unions. History is replete with examples of national governments winning over the opponents, and much of the progress that has been made since 1945 can be credited to initiatives such as the General Agreement on Tariffs and Trade (GATT), replaced in 1995 by the World Trade Organization (WTO). But no part of the world has made so much progress on this front as Europe, whose achievements mean – ironically – that it is less often compared favourably to those parts of the world that continue to protect their markets than unfavourably to the open market of the United States. As more is achieved, it seems, so more is expected.

It is somewhat easier to speculate about what a country would lose should it leave the European Union. While it would still have access to many of the opportunities of the single market, it would not have the advantage of being involved in making decisions or shaping the development of that market. It would be a less compelling destination for companies based overseas or in the EU, since it would be outside the European marketplace. It might be freed from many of the regulations that come with EU membership, but many of those regulations have been good for business and consumers, and advantageous to those doing trade within the EU. It would lose most of the subsidies that come with membership of the EU and participation in projects such as the Common Agricultural Policy, tariffs on trade in many products (particularly food and trade) would grow, new arrangements would have to be made for nationals living in other EU states and nationals of those states living in the departed state, and the trade agreements reached over many years between the EU and other parts of the world would need to be replaced with a host of new bilateral agreements, which might not have such favourable terms.[14]

The Euro

Given its myriad recent woes, it is hard to find many today who have much good to say about the euro. But let us not forget that during its first decade, it was doing quite well – travellers and consumers were content, business was happy, there was public and political support in every euro zone state for the single currency, which was even being described in some quarters as a threat to the global dominance of the US dollar. And for those who have been able to maintain a steady nerve during the euro zone crisis, there has been a silver lining: the crisis has obliged euro zone governments to work to address several critical design problems with the euro, has obliged several EU governments to fix structural problems in their economies, and has brought the debate over Europe to a much wider audience. This is not an ideal scenario, but let us not forget Monnet's law from Chapter 1: people only accept change when they are faced with necessity, and only recognize necessity when a crisis is upon them. Not always true, perhaps, but certainly true in this case.

The need for a single European currency was long part of the conversation about the single market, the first efforts to achieve exchange rate stability dating back to the late 1950s. There were two false starts in the early 1970s and the 1980s, and long-held concerns about how a single currency might erode national sovereignty, reduce the ability of national governments to address different economic cycles and varying levels of poverty, and possibly cause problems in one state to spill over into problems in another. But governments proceeded, the euro was launched in January 1999, and the final abolition of participating national currencies took place in early 2002. There was optimism that even in the face of public doubts about its adoption, the euro would be the capstone of the single market project.

It is also important to remember that the creation of the euro was as much a political initiative as an economic venture; its introduction, noted German foreign minister Joschka Fischer at the time, 'was not only the crowning-point of economic integration, it was also a profoundly political act, because a currency is not just another economic factor but also symbolizes the power of the sovereign who guarantees it'.[15] Monetary policy in western Europe prior to the launch of economic and monetary union was very much subject to the lead of the German central bank, but the world's dominant currency since the 1950s has been the US dollar. While sustainable economic and monetary policies in the United States would have posed few problems for Europeans, the unilateral decision by the US to break the final links between the dollar and gold in 1971 caused many misgivings in Europe, and American economic leadership has become increasingly unsteady since the late 1990s with a ballooning national debt, lavish spending on two wars of questionable merit, and the inadequacies of regulation that helped spawn the global financial crisis.

While considerable care was taken to define the terms of membership of the euro zone and the responsibilities of the European Central Bank, and the early years of the euro gave much cause for confidence, there were also early signs of problems. Greece had been allowed to join the euro even though it had not met the budget deficit levels set as a condition of entry, and it became clear in 2002–3 that recession was making it difficult for several euro states to meet the terms of membership, such as limits on borrowing. Those terms were the brainchild of Germany, which, ironically, was the first to break them, joined later by France and Italy, while Greece continued to lie heroically about its financial situation. But government borrowing was less of a problem than irresponsible private sector borrowing, which – encouraged by low interest rates – generated an economic boom fuelled by debt in Spain and Italy.

The global financial crisis broke in late 2007, creating pressures that spilled over into the euro zone and in late 2009 revealed the extent of Greece's misbehaviour. There were fears that Greece's problems might be contagious; questions were asked about prospects for Portugal, Ireland, Spain and even Italy (again fuelled more by the private sector than by Greek-style government profligacy); EU leaders were found wanting in their ability to either fully understand or respond to the crisis; the Merkel government was constrained by domestic considerations to move slowly in providing leadership; and there was speculation that some countries might have to leave the euro zone. The future of the euro was now questioned, with suggestions that the entire European project might be about to collapse.

The years since the breaking of the euro zone crisis have been a wild ride, to be sure, and it is easy and tempting with the wisdom of hindsight to point to the euro as exemplifying the potential costs of EU states giving up too much control over economic policy, or as underlining the problems of moving into new policy territory without adequate understanding of the implications or sufficient institutional safeguards. But several key points are worth remembering:

- Although some of the euro's problems have been the result of design flaws (particularly the lack of a centralized means of monitoring spending and borrowing in its member states), most have been the result of a combination of bad decisions, political hesitancy and misfortune. Had Greece been barred entry to the euro zone and had the euro zone states respected their own rules on spending and borrowing, the story might have been quite different. And had the global financial crisis not come when it did, euro zone states might have been able to deal with the structural problems of the euro in a more considered fashion, without the distraction of alarm bells of crisis ringing loudly in their ears.
- Confidence in the euro may have plummeted in 2010–11, and euro zone leaders may have dithered in their response, but they

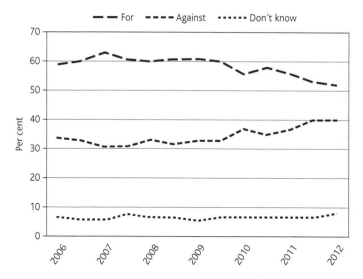

Source: European Commission, *Eurobarometer* 77 (Spring 2012), First Results, 15. Opinion on a European economic and monetary union with a single currency, the euro.

Figure 2   Public opinion on the euro

were sailing uncharted territory and playing as much as anything to domestic electorates. That even the best political and economic brains did not fully understand the mechanics of the euro was revealed in 2012 when efforts to impose austerity on several EU states began to be counterproductive, and there was a switch to an emphasis on efforts to promote growth.

- The European public has remained in favour of the euro by large margins (see Figure 2). Supporters outnumbered opponents by two to one between 2002 and 2009, even as the EU enlarged from 17 to 27 members. Just before the Greek crisis broke, supporters outnumbered opponents in every EU country except the UK, and even with the breaking of the crisis there was still majority support across the EU. There was still 52 per cent support for the euro in euro zone states in the spring of 2012, and when asked which entity was best placed to take action against the effects of the financial and economic crisis, as many Europeans opted for the EU as for their national governments.[16]

- Governments did not significantly reduce their holdings of euros during the crisis, and nor was there much talk among prospective members of changing their plans to join: Slovakia joined in January 2009, Estonia joined in January 2011, and there were few signs in remaining eastern European EU member states of serious second thoughts. Of the EU states still outside the euro zone, public and political resistance to joining remained significant only in Britain, Denmark and Sweden.

A June 2011 survey found that the view that the euro had been bad for national economies was strongest in two countries that did not have the euro (Sweden and the UK), while opinions in Germany, Italy and the Netherlands were about evenly split.[17]

Above all, it is important to remember the manifold advantages of the euro. Without it, travellers would still be subject to all those costly and annoying exchange problems that remain the bane of visits to countries with different currencies. Being able to shop in different countries using the same currency allows them to make more direct comparisons of costs, and there is an important psychological element to the euro: few things make us feel more foreign when we are travelling than having to use different currencies, while the availability of the euro at home and abroad helps make the foreign seem more familiar. Business has long been a champion of the single currency because it removes transaction costs, removes concerns about having to plan for changes in exchange rates, opens up new commercial opportunities, and promotes trade and foreign investment by removing the problems of companies and governments having to deal in different currencies.

We should also remember the political significance of the euro, which remains just as true now as it did a decade ago. The euro is the only serious competitor to the US dollar as a major world currency (the Japanese yen coming a distant third and the Chinese yuan so far behind as to be almost invisible), and the economic woes of the United States may yet do lasting long-term damage to the dollar and play into the hands of the euro. To suggest, as some have, that in the German Deutschmark and the British pound the Europeans already had two perfectly adequate global currencies is to be in denial; they

Box 5: Nine reasons why we need the euro

1. Cross-border travel without the need to exchange currencies, pay transaction fees or worry about fluctuations in exchange rates.
2. Greater transparency that allows consumers to more easily compare prices.
3. Greater ease for businesses to find suppliers offering goods or services at lower prices, thereby bringing down costs and improving competition.
4. Eased transaction of cross-border business, with less concern about the risks posed by fluctuations in exchange rates, which can eat into profits.
5. A new incentive for foreign businesses to trade with and invest in the EU.
6. The promotion of exports through the removal of foreign exchange uncertainties.
7. Important psychological effects, helping make the foreign seem more familiar to Europeans, and removing one of the most persistent reminders of the differences among European states.
8. The provision for euro zone states of a more clearly vested interest in the economic welfare of its partners.
9. The provision of a world-class currency that places the euro zone in a stronger position to compete with the US dollar, with concomitant political advantages.

were both small players in a club dominated by the dollar. Not only would the single market be handicapped without an effective single currency, but a stable euro remains critical to any claims that the EU is a global economic leader.

The problems of the euro will not go away any time soon, and making judgements about its prospects while those problems remain unresolved is dangerous. Nonetheless, the effects of design flaws, poor domestic economic policy choices, excessive private sector borrowing, and the unfortunate timing of the global financial crisis should not let us lose sight of the benefits of bringing EU economies together with a single currency. Financial trends are in large part about confidence, and much of the lack of confidence in the euro of late has stemmed from its being a currency without a state and without the institutional paraphernalia and bonds of solidarity that a state would have.[18]

Numerous scenarios have been proposed for the future of the euro, the range – from the upbeat and optimistic to the gloomy and pessimistic – reflecting the extent to which economists and political leaders are making educated guesses, and muddling through as developments unfold. One of those scenarios is that the necessary fiscal and structural reforms are made, the response to the crisis works, confidence in the euro is restored, the EU learns from its mistakes, the euro emerges in a stronger position, the years of crisis become an increasingly distant if deeply unpleasant memory, and we remember once again why it was created. As an alternative to continuing to muddle through, or to abandoning the euro, with all the political and economic shock waves that would result, this is by far the preferable option.

4 Europe as a Democracy

The EU is often criticized for being elitist and undemocratic, and for being run by technocrats who are out of touch with the needs and views of ordinary Europeans. Scholars have spent much time pondering what they describe as its democratic deficit, or the gap between the work of the EU institutions and the ability of ordinary Europeans to have a say in that work. Such is the problem that a member of the British parliament was once prompted to quip that if the EU applied for membership of itself, it would be denied on the grounds that it lacked the necessary democratic credentials.[1] There is a popular perception that the EU institutions are unaccountable, which is why the comments section of online stories about the EU will often find it described as 'an unelected, unaccountable, corrupt monolith with an overbearing bureaucracy' (or words to that effect).

But herein lie several of the numerous paradoxes about the EU. First, it is criticized for being undemocratic, and yet the most obvious solution – the creation of an elected and representative European government – is vigorously and widely opposed. Second, Europeans have been turning their back in growing numbers on their one clear and obvious opportunity to affect EU decision making: elections to the European Parliament. And finally, as noted before, it is often the elites themselves who dismiss the EU as elitist. Meanwhile, polls tell us that large majorities of Europeans think of the EU as both democratic and modern, feel a sense of belonging to the EU, and have greater trust in the EU institutions than in their own national government institutions.

One of the problems with discussing democracy is that it has numerous qualities that are hard to measure, such that almost any society can claim to be democratic if the definition is pushed far enough. Indeed, no rational government would admit to being undemocratic, and the loudest claims of democracy often come from those governments that are least democratic according to the conventional definition of the term (to the extent that we can agree such a thing). Conversely, democracy in practice has enough structural flaws that doubts are regularly cast on the responsiveness even of those countries most widely acclaimed as democracies, including every one of the member states of the EU.

In other words, democracy is messy, inconsistent and complicated, it often disappoints, it never lives up to its ideal of universal equality, and, as Winston Churchill once said, it is the worst form of government except for all the others. Democracies may have constitutions and laws and elected representatives with carefully prescribed powers, but they are never entirely inclusive, many of their citizens feel left out or overlooked, the flaws in their designs are constantly being tinkered with, and human nature means that there will never be a perfect system of government in which all are equally involved and equally protected. In this regard, then, questions about the democratic credentials of the EU are quite normal and fully to be expected.

But as to how we understand those credentials, much depends on how we understand the EU. If it is a federal United States of Europe, which patently it is not, then there are problems. Only the European Parliament could be considered a democratic institution according to conventional understandings of the requirements of representation; all other EU institutions are only indirectly accountable through the governments of the member states (note, however, that they *are* accountable). But if the EU is a confederation, then its democratic credentials are as would be expected: citizen interests are represented indirectly at the European level through the governments of the member states, and the EU is a union of states rather than a union of citizens.

But whatever we choose to call the EU, its institutions are more accountable and responsive than the critics would have us believe. As we saw in Chapter 1, the European Council and the Council of the EU consist of elected national leaders, who must answer for their actions and decisions at national elections. The European Parliament is directly elected by European voters, who have the opportunity every five years to cast ballots designed to keep Parliament responsive. And the appointment of the commissioners who run the European Commission and the judges who run the Court of Justice is controlled by the member states, providing Europeans with another layer of indirect representation. The American political scientist Andrew Moravcsik suggests that while the EU may not be an 'ideal' parliamentary democracy, it is legitimate, its institutions are tightly constrained by checks and balances, and concerns about the democratic deficit are misplaced.[2]

There is more. The EU is founded on treaties, or agreements under international law entered into between sovereign states, committing all parties to shared obligations, with any failure to meet them being considered a breach of the agreement. The steps taken to develop and adopt those treaties have often been sloppy, achieving absurdist qualities in the three instances where the voters 'got it wrong' the first time and were asked to vote again (Denmark on Maastricht, and Ireland on Nice and Lisbon). Nonetheless, the treaties still stand as the basic rule book of Europe, are the functional equivalent of a European constitution, and keep everyone reasonably honest and accountable.

Let us also not forget that European integration has contributed to both a widening of the definition of human rights, and a deepening of their protection. Consider the work of the Council of Europe, the oldest of the major European institutions (founded in 1949) and one of whose earliest projects was the drawing up of the European Convention on Human Rights, which entered into force in 1953. Sidelined until human rights moved up the European agenda in the 1990s, and the European Court of Human Rights became a permanent institution in 1998, the convention is today part of the legal framework of the European project and a channel for the promotion of human rights in all 47 member states of the Council of Europe, including Russia.

It can also be said that one of the primary achievements of European integration has been to deepen and widen the reach of democracy. It is hard to remember from our modern vantage point how many doubts there were about how the political record of Europe might evolve after the Second World War: German and Italian government had to be rebuilt almost from scratch, the shadow of Soviet authoritarianism had expanded over much of the east (posing threats also to the west), and dictatorship persisted in Portugal and Spain. From a core foundation in north-western Europe, however, democracy regained its traction and improved on its earlier achievements, and European integration was critical to the process; it provided the shared project that kept Europeans talking to each other, and later expanded the reach of democracy with the demands it made of aspirant members; membership of the EU is open only to countries that are democratic, that have functioning free markets, and that can take on the obligations of the existing body of laws and regulations adopted by the EU (known as the *acquis communautaire*). The EU also stands, as we have seen, as a civilian actor that encourages democracy and human rights globally by wielding carrots rather than sticks.

In short, the EU is more democratic than the critics would have us believe, it has been a compelling force for democratic and free market change, and the major reason it does not measure up well to the kind of representative democracy practised in its member states is because many Europeans choose not to exploit the opportunities made available to them to make their voices heard. Eurosceptics are particularly critical of its performance and yet are also quickest to resist even minimalist efforts to more clearly define the channels of responsibility in today's EU, let alone maximalist efforts to take European integration any further. Europe, then, exists by default in a limbo where its administrative structure moves neither forwards nor backwards. Were we to acknowledge the EU for being a European confederation, we could set out to better understand how confederations work, using the EU's channels of representation more effectively, better understanding the public role of its senior officials, and – by doing so – encouraging them more actively to listen to European public opinion and to use their offices to better define and articulate European interests.

What Do Europeans Think of the EU?

One measure of the health of a democracy is the strength of the association between public opinion and the actions of political representatives and the governing institutions of which they are a part. Candidates for office routinely claim to have the best interests of voters at heart and to be willing to follow the wishes of voters, but the wishes of voters are many and varied, and not always easy to determine. In order to better understand how well or badly the European project fits with the wishes of Europeans we must first understand what they think of the EU. The polling data make two key points:

- Most Europeans support the EU, feel that it has brought benefits to their countries, and feel a sense of belonging to the EU. Support has tailed off in the wake of the global financial and euro zone crises, but not to the point where the foundations of the European project appear to have been questioned by most people. Most of the media analysis, unfortunately, tells us quite the opposite.
- Most Europeans do not understand the EU. This begs the obvious question of how they can support it if they do not understand it, but the same paradox applies at the national level: few Europeans take an active ongoing interest in public affairs or could explain in much detail how their national systems of government work, or talk with much authority about most key policy problems, and yet they continue to instinctively support the national political systems by which they are governed (even if they do not always admire the holders of elective offices).

The best source of data on European public opinion over an extended period of time is the series of biannual polls carried out since 1974 by Eurobarometer, a European Commission-sponsored polling service. The problems of opinion polling are well known; there are examples of national polls which sometimes challenge the findings of Eurobarometer polls, and eurosceptics might question the credibility of studies undertaken and funded by the institution they most like to castigate. But Eurobarometer is an independent service and its pollsters are adept at posing sound questions, constructing representative samples, and drawing conclusions which are often blunt and forthright about the state of opinion on the EU.

When asked what they think of the effects of EU membership on their home country, a steady majority of Europeans over the last decade (just over a half in most polls) has been of the view that membership has benefited their country, while only about one-third feel that their country has not benefited (see Figure 3). Levels of support and opposition have not fluctuated much in spite of the growth in membership of the European club and in spite of the political and economic problems experienced by the EU and the wider

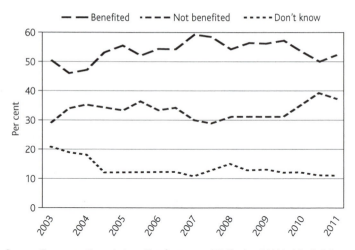

Source: European Commission, *Eurobarometer* 75 (Spring 2011), 34. Opinion on extent to which home country has benefited or not benefited from EU membership.

Figure 3 What Europeans think of EU membership

world. As the euro zone crisis deepened there was an increase in the number of Europeans who saw no benefits for their country, but they were still outnumbered by those who saw benefits.

When asked about their image of the EU, those with positive views of the EU outnumbered those with negative views by three to one (roughly 45 per cent to 15 per cent) until the breaking of the euro zone crisis; by early 2012, only 31 per cent thought positively about the EU compared to 28 per cent who thought negatively, while 39 per cent were neutral.[3] Of course, it is impossible to determine from these data what drives the changing positive/negative ratio. Did it reflect a growing rejection of the EU and/or European integration, was it a function of the confused response to the crisis from European leaders, was it a comment on the particular troubles of the euro, was it reflective of the general economic downturn in Europe, had more Europeans been influenced by the gloomy media coverage of the euro zone crisis, or were there other factors at play?

On the EU's democratic credentials, about two-thirds of Europeans consider the EU to be democratic and modern, compared to about a quarter who do not, while slightly less than half think of it as technocratic.[4] On the matter of trust, more Europeans than not had faith in EU institutions until the breaking of the euro zone crisis, since when distrusters have outnumbered trusters by about 2–5 percentage points.[5] But faith in national institutions has not been strong of late either; Eurobarometer found between 2004 and 2011 that trust in the EU consistently ran about 13–18 points higher than trust in national government, opinion about both falling to all-time lows in 2012: 31 per cent trusted the EU while only 28 per cent trusted their national governments.[6]

It is interesting to note that while 40 per cent of Europeans thought that matters were headed in the wrong direction in the EU in early 2011, 44 per cent thought that matters were headed in the wrong direction in the world, and 51 per cent in their home countries.[7] The problem here, then, lies less with the EU specifically than with government, administration and economic matters more generally. And if we think the story is bad in Europe, spare a moment to consider the worries of Americans: polls in the United States during 2011–12 revealed that as many as four out of five Americans thought their country was headed in the wrong direction.[8] Particular criticism is directed at Congress, the political institution that is considered closest to the daily needs of Americans and yet which is so bitterly divided, and whose members place short-term local interests so patently above long-term national interests, that it is hamstrung by partisan opinion. Compared to Americans, it seems that Europeans are in fact quite optimistic about the future.

When it comes to opinions on specific policy initiatives by the EU, Europeans are strongly supportive of a common defence and security policy (75 per cent in favour, 17 per cent opposed) and of a common foreign policy (64 per cent in favour, 26 per cent opposed). Most remarkably, there was majority support for the euro even in 2012 as its problems were clearly worsening (52 per cent in favour, 40 per cent opposed). In only one of the four policy areas tested – further enlargement of the EU – has opposition outweighed support,[9] and in spite of the trials of the EU and the euro, the autumn 2011 Eurobarometer poll found that 58 per cent were optimistic about the future of the EU while only 36 per cent were pessimistic.[10]

But against the background of all these data, the polls also emphasize the problem of the knowledge deficit: most Europeans do

---

Box 6: What do Europeans think of the EU?

- Just over half believe EU membership has been a good thing, while about one-third think it has been a bad thing.
- Before the euro zone crisis, three times as many had a positive image of the EU as had a negative image.
- Two-thirds think of the EU as democratic and modern, while about a quarter do not.
- More have trust in EU institutions than in national government institutions.
- Those who were optimistic about the future of the EU in 2011 outnumbered pessimists by 58 per cent to 36 per cent.
- More Europeans think their country is headed in the wrong direction than think the EU is headed in the wrong direction (51 per cent to 40 per cent).
- 75 per cent favour a common defence and security policy, and support for the euro continues to outweigh opposition.
- Most admit that they do not understand the EU and how it works.

---

not understand how the EU works and cannot see how it affects their lives. Eurobarometer surveys have periodically asked respondents to score themselves on how much they think they know about the EU, and have occasionally asked them factual questions designed to test their knowledge. On a scale of 1 to 10, with a 1 meaning that they knew nothing about the EU and a 10 meaning that they knew a great deal, about one-fifth of respondents in the late 1990s and early 2000s gave themselves a score of 1 or 2, about half gave themselves scores of between 3 and 5, and only 2 per cent placed themselves at the top of the class with a score of 9 or 10.[11] In other words, more than two-thirds of Europeans gave themselves a failing score of 5 or less.

The poll has since been structured differently, asking people simply how much they think they know about the EU, and the results have been much the same: in a 2010 poll, only 32 per cent considered themselves well informed on European issues, against 66 per cent who did not, while in a 2011 poll, only 42 per cent thought they understood how the EU worked.[12] Men claimed to be better

informed than women by 40 to 26 per cent, higher levels of education and higher self-placement on the social scale correlated with
better knowledge, managers considered themselves better informed
than workers, and there was not much difference by age.

These data measure how much people *think* they know, which
raises the obvious question of how they can know how much they
know if they don't know much. Eurobarometer addresses this problem by posing simple factual questions designed to test how much
people actually know, and the results are not encouraging. Only 45
per cent in 2007 knew that Members of the European Parliament
were directly elected (a proportion that had grown to 56 per cent by
2011),[13] while barely half knew in 2007 that the EU had 15 member
states (by 2011, two-thirds knew that it had 27 members).[14] One of
the most persistent myths about the EU relates to how much it costs,
most people wildly overestimating the numbers. When Britons were
asked in 2009 how much their country contributed to the EU budget
as a percentage of gross national income, the average estimate
among the half who offered an answer was 23 per cent. The actual
figure was 0.2 per cent.[15]

Voter ignorance is not unique to the EU, and has been a matter of
worried debate among scholars, philosophers and political leaders
dating back to the time of the ancient Greeks. Since the early 1990s
there has been a popular theory that doubtful or confused voters
make up for their knowledge shortfall by relying on cues from the
political leaders and parties with which they identify, on media
coverage of politics, and to some extent on the work of interest
groups.[16] This supposedly allows them to make a 'reasoned choice'
or to act 'as if' they were informed. But in the case of the EU, this
theory has at least two fatal flaws. First, the EU is often criticized for
its elitist qualities, and yet here we have the suggestion that listening
to those elites is one way of getting around the knowledge deficit.
Second, we must consider the effects of confirmation bias: most
people tend to listen only to those politicians and media sources with
which they agree, making them less able to think independently
about the pros and cons of the EU. The cues, in short, do not help
create an informed and independently minded electorate so much as
confirm people in their predispositions.

At the same time, we are being swamped with information,
making it difficult to keep up, and to decide what is important and

what is not. The internet has made volumes available at the click of a mouse, but it has also brought information overload, made it more difficult to sort the wheat from the chaff (or the signal from the noise, as the pollster Nate Silver puts it[17]), and encouraged fragmentation as many of us try to maintain some sense of order and control by looking only to those sources that fit with our view of the world. Harvard law professor Cass Sunstein notes the role of the internet in expanding our horizons, but also warns that many people are using it for the opposite function, 'creating a *Daily Me* that is specifically tailored to their own interests and prejudices'. He argues that a well-functioning democracy 'depends not just on freedom from censorship, but also on a set of common experiences and on unsought, unanticipated, and even unwanted exposures to diverse topics, people, and ideas'. A system of information 'gated communities' or 'echo chambers', he argues, is unhealthy for public discourse.[18]

The challenge we face, then, is twofold. First, how do we encourage Europeans to learn more about the EU? This is a tough one, which exercises the EU institutions a great deal. It is hard to have constructive discussions about the EU unless we are each armed with at least a modicum of understanding about how it works and what it means, ideally unpolluted by the spin placed on that understanding by its more ardent supporters and its opponents. But not everyone is interested enough in the European project to invest the time in keeping up, and even if there was some magic formula for engaging more people in public affairs, most would be more interested in local or national politics because they have more immediate effects. To find a formula that would spark wider interest in Europe, then, is that much more difficult. (I do take a stab, however, in Chapter 8.)

Second, how do we encourage Europeans to consider competing views on the EU so that they improve their chances of developing reasonably informed and balanced opinions? As information consumers we are all looking for shortcuts and easy options, and find it more comforting to have our predispositions supported rather than challenged. Whether we have made up our minds on an issue through detailed research, or whether we have opinions based more on instinct (or prompted by the media and experts that we trust), it is easier and quicker to dismiss the arguments of the opposition out of hand than to give them more considered attention. Which leads us to the bigger question of how many opportunities are available for Europeans to engage with the work of the EU.

Channels for Democratic Expression in the EU

As we have seen, the EU is not a federal superstate and so does not have the standard qualities of a representative democracy; most obviously, none of its 'leaders' (such as the presidents of the European Council and the European Commission) are directly elected. But this is not – as more hardened eurosceptics suggest – because of deliberate attempts to control and obfuscate so much as because of the hesitancy that the governments of the member states have displayed in taking the steps that would convert the EU from an international organization writ large into a more formalized system of shared governance. But just because the EU is neither one thing nor the other, this does not mean that it lacks democratic credentials. On the contrary, there are many ways in which Europeans can express their views on EU matters and at the same time have their political choices widened and their personal freedoms better protected.

We can begin with the treaties. All democracies have constitutions whose purposes include listing the goals and aspirations of a state (such as democracy, freedom and human rights), outlining the powers and responsibilities of government, establishing the limits on the powers of government, and spelling out the rights of the governed. The EU lacks a constitution in the conventional sense of the term, although it tried in 2003–5 to develop one, a project that was brought to an end by a negative referendum vote in France. Instead it has operated on the basis of a series of treaties, each one amending those that came before.

While this is not an ideal situation, the treaties are the functional equivalent of a constitution. Strictly speaking, they are agreements among governments rather than compacts between people and their governments, but little matter: they do almost everything that is normally expected of constitutions, telling us about the goals and purposes of the EU, the operational rules and powers of its institutions, and the general principles of integration as well as more detailed rules and obligations. So anyone who has questions or doubts about what the EU can and cannot do has a set of rules and guiding principles to which they can refer. The treaties do not always make for light or easy reading, but this is what happens when you give drafting responsibilities to committees and take into account the opinions and perspectives of multiple different interests.

And if this is not protection enough, the European Court of Justice is there to make sure that the rules of the EU are applied correctly and to provide interpretation of those rules where questions are raised. Ironically, and in spite of the Court's critical role in giving the work of the EU consistency and legitimacy, it is the least well known of the EU's major institutions, and it is hard to know what Europeans think of it; Eurobarometer polls thoughtfully ask Europeans if they have heard of Parliament, the Commission and the European Council (large majorities have) and whether or not they trust them (trust has fallen in conjunction with falling trust in government more generally), but do not think to ask about opinion of the Court (although there is a strand of eurosceptic thought that charges the Court with having been one of the most active promoters of integration). Its workload nonetheless continues to grow, suggesting that many are taking advantage of its interpretive services.

In terms of direct channels of democratic representation made available at the EU level to Europeans, the most important and fundamental is offered by elections to the European Parliament (EP). There is nothing particularly unusual about these; they serve the same function as elections to national or local legislatures, with all eligible EU voters offered the opportunity every five years to elect representatives to the EP, choosing from among a wide array of national political parties that have been improving their links with like-minded parties in other EU states. At the same time, Parliament has become a more substantial body with growing powers over the European law-making process; it cannot directly introduce proposals for new laws (those come from the Commission) but it can amend laws and it shares authority with the Council of the EU for the final vote on enactment of new laws.

In spite of this, and in spite of complaints about the lack of democracy and transparency in EU institutions, turnout at EP elections has been falling since their introduction in 1979. That first year, when there were only nine member states in what was then the EEC, a respectable 62 per cent of voters turned out. At the elections in 2009, by which time membership of the EU had climbed to 27, just

43 per cent turned out. Multiple explanations have been offered for this decline,[19] the most compelling being that the stakes in EP elections are lower than those in national elections; there is no change of government at stake and the outcome does not make an obvious difference in the lives of EU voters. This raises another paradox in the debate about the EU: it is charged by critics with being too powerful and for reducing the independence of its member states, and yet most voters do not think that elections to the EP (the only directly elected EU institution) are sufficiently important for them to make the small investment of time to vote.

We should also not forget the place of national elections in holding the EU accountable. Europe tends not to rank high in the list of considerations that most Europeans bring to their decisions on national government, but this does not mean that national political parties can ignore it altogether; their position on Europe has impacted numerous mainstream parties, and recent decades have seen the rise of parties based almost entirely on the question of Europe (or, more accurately, on their hostility to Europe). This presents us with the interesting sight of parties campaigning to win seats in the European Parliament, the very institution they would like to see abolished, which suggests that they believe the EP must have some authority and ability to get things done. National elections also offer us another glimpse into the confederal qualities of the EU; they are designed to choose the governments that then go on to represent national interests at the European level.

A second channel through which voters can make their views heard on European matters is the national referendum. More than 40 of these have been held to date, more than half of them since 1998, and most of them asking for public views on membership of the EU or the euro, or on the adoption of a new treaty. They are far from perfect as a democratic tool, not least because there is no consistency regarding when or under what circumstances they will be held; more than a third of them have been held in just two countries (Ireland and Denmark), while seven EU member states (including Germany) have never had a referendum on an EU question. And the evidence suggests not only that many voters are not clear about the issues at stake, but also that they will often cast their ballots not on the question on the ballot so much as on the basis of their opinion about the incumbent national government.

Take the example of the critical 2005 French vote on the European constitutional treaty: a Eurobarometer poll carried out at the time found that 74 per cent of French citizens had either heard of the treaty but knew 'very little' about its contents, or had not heard of it at all,[20] and yet 69 per cent of voters turned out, of whom just under 55 per cent rejected the treaty. It was later speculated that the result was not only a reflection of dissatisfaction with the treaty and with the direction being taken by European integration, but also of hostility to the incumbent Chirac administration, and of the widening gap between political leaders and citizens in France.[21] In spite of the problems of referendums, they are among Europe's few experiences with direct democracy at the national level, most public discussion about them revolves around complaints that there are too few rather than too many, and they have the advantage of drawing public attention in selected countries to European issues.

Box 7: Eight channels for the protection of public interests in the EU

1. The treaties of the EU, which spell out the powers and responsibilities of the EU institutions.
2. Judgments of the European Court of Justice, which help clarify the meaning and the reach of EU law.
3. Elections to the European Parliament, the only directly elected EU institution.
4. National elections, when EU matters are often on the agendas of competing parties.
5. National referendums on EU questions.
6. The work of interest groups, which promote and defend the agendas of broad economic and social groups or more focused special interests.
7. Complaints lodged with the European Ombudsman, or suggestions for new laws under the citizen initiative.
8. The Charter of Fundamental Rights of the EU, and the European Convention on Human Rights, the latter supported by the European Court of Human Rights.

Less often appreciated by most Europeans as a channel for representation are the efforts of an expanding network of interest groups that work with the EU institutions to represent their constituencies, to provide expert information, and to keep an eye on the performance of national governments in meeting their legal obligations. As the reach and significance of EU law and policy has grown, so has the number of groups that have opened offices in Brussels and built links with the EU institutions, particularly the Commission and the European Parliament. Just how many there are is hard to say, one estimate in 2008 placing the number of groups organized to work at the European level at just over 850,[22] but the total number of groups with offices in Brussels now runs well into the thousands. Most represent business and labour interests (among them Business Europe, the European Consumers Organization, and the European Trade Union Confederation), while the balance represent mainly public interests and the professions.

Opinion on the work of interest groups is divided. One view holds that they are valuable channels through which the interests of defined sectors in society can be expressed to policymakers, while another holds that they promote elitism and unfair advantages by offering those sectors fast-track access; the wealthier and better organized the groups, and the more powerful the sectors they represent, the more skewed the results. But if groups are a key and inevitable part of democratic discourse within the member states, it is natural that they would follow the lines of decision making, which in this case have taken them to Brussels. A stroll around the European Quarter in that city will not only take visitors past the major EU institutions but past office blocks displaying lists of tenants representing everything from regions and provinces within the member states to a wide range of economic, social and more defined interests, as well as think-tanks that debate European issues and share their analyses of what is right and what is wrong with the European project. This is another sign of healthy engagement with public issues.

Other, less telling, formal channels for expression include the office of the European Ombudsman, where complaints can be lodged about maladministration in any of the EU institutions (except the Court of Justice). Anyone who is a citizen or legal resident of the EU can lodge a complaint, which might be about discrimination, abuse of power, failure to fulfil responsibilities or delays in taking action. And a more recent and so far only modestly tested option is the citizen initiative, by which anyone who can gather a million signatures may ask the European Commission to develop a new law in an area of interest. The topics of the earliest initiatives included proposals for laws to stop scientific experiments on animals, to give EU citizens living in other EU states the right to vote in national elections, to provide more funds for student exchanges, and to end roaming fees throughout the EU (a goal that has now been achieved).

Human Rights and the EU

That Europe does not end with the work of the EU and its institutions is illustrated most clearly by the role of the Council of Europe and its most important creation, the European Court of Human Rights (both of them based in Strasbourg in France). Their activities have helped expand the protection of human rights, the implications being felt not just within the EU but across Europe more widely; both organizations have 47 member states, including Russia and every European country except Belarus and Kosovo. And their influence does not stop there, because the reach of European standards has been felt in countries outside Europe, which have been obliged to meet European demands in order to continue doing political and economic business with Europe.

The first statement of rights in post-war Europe was contained in the European Convention on Human Rights, drawn up in 1950 by the Council of Europe and entering into force in 1953; signature of the convention has since been a requirement for any country joining the Council. Focusing on civil and political rights, and standing as one of the most thorough and detailed outlines of human rights ever agreed, the convention did not have much bite until the EU in the 1990s began to require respect for human rights as a condition for the entry of new members, and more effective monitoring of human rights was seen as part of the solution to the post-Maastricht backlash against integration.[23] When the European Court of Human Rights (ECHR) became a permanent institution in 1998, the right of petition to the Court became more widely known, and its workload grew.

The Court has gone on to rule on cases involving human rights abuses, discrimination, the improper conduct of trials and the mistreatment of prisoners. In 2000, the UK was obliged to end its ban on openly gay men and women serving in the armed forces in response to an ECHR ruling. The Court found Russia guilty of human rights abuses in Chechnya in 2005, and Bosnia of discriminating against Jews and Roma in 2009; in 2005 it judged the British ban on allowing prisoners to vote in elections to be a violation of their rights, and in 2010 upheld a complaint against a British anti-terror law allowing police to stop and search people without firm grounds for suspicion. It has issued rulings on torture or police brutality against Russia, Ukraine, Turkey and Romania, and it has several times addressed the matter of the gap between church and state, including a ruling in 2009 against the hanging of crucifixes in Italian classrooms. Turkey and Italy have topped the list of violators brought before the Court, many of the Turkish cases involving the right to a fair trial and the protection of property, and many of the Italian cases involving the excessive length of legal proceedings.[24]

That the Court has filled a much-needed niche is reflected in the immensity of its workload: during its first 30 years it received fewer than 800 applications per year and issued fewer than 70 judgements, but in the ten years after becoming permanent it received an annual average of 45,000 applications.[25] By the end of 2009 it had a backlog of appeals that would have taken nearly half a century to clear at its existing pace of work, sparking reforms in 2010 that included reducing the number of judges involved in hearing a case.

Critics have charged the Court with providing too many rights to criminals, but the criticisms as often as not stem from efforts to dilute the reach of European institutions, and are often politically motivated rather than being based on matters of law and human rights. Britain has again been one of the leaders of the eurosceptic pack, calling for changes to the Court that would limit access to those facing human rights violations. The interest group Human Rights Watch has described British moves as serving 'the interests of governments over those of the potential victims of human rights violations'.[26] The Convention and the Court are examples of how standards and expectations can be raised by countries working together rather than in isolation.

Rights are also at the heart of the Charter of Fundamental Rights of the European Union, adopted in 2000 and brought into force with the Treaty of Lisbon. Not so much a new initiative as a gathering of rights already recognized by EU member states into a single document, the Charter addresses the right to life (confirming the abolition of the death penalty throughout the EU); the right to physical and mental integrity; protection against torture and slavery; respect for private and family life; protection of personal data; freedom of thought and religion; freedom of expression and association; the right to marriage, education, work, property, asylum, equality, health care, social security, free movement and residence; respect for cultural diversity; the right to a fair trial; rights for children, the elderly, the disabled and workers; and expectations about environmental and consumer protection.

The debate about rights is long and contentious, with differences of opinion about – on the one hand – natural or universal human rights (which are routinely breached or ignored by authoritarian governments, raising questions about their universality) and – on the other hand – rights established by law. There are also criticisms that what we know as universal rights have been defined mainly by western liberal culture and that they do not pay enough heed to the diversity of human society. This has been a problem in the debate over multiculturalism, and over whether the traditions of one society that other societies may find unacceptable should be recognized and allowed for. In other words, are rights universal or merely local?

The effect of the European approach to rights has been to see them defined and protected communally rather than by states working in isolation. The same kind of leader/laggard pressures (discussed in Chapter 6) that have been behind the strengthening of standards apply also to rights; states and communities with weaker records will be compelled to change their records through peer pressure and the desire to be part of a larger community with the same safeguards and expectations. The EU also has a greater chance of flexing its soft influence if its member states are agreed on the rights they accord their citizens.

5 Europe as a Community

To have a shared purpose and identity is difficult without a sense of community, and on this front the European project has much still to do. 'We have created Europe,' the Polish historian Bronislaw Geremek once quipped (borrowing from the Italian patriot Garibaldi). 'Now we have to create Europeans.' But what is a European? This is a question often posed but rarely answered, and the lack of an answer, coupled with the seeming lack of a sense of community, is often cited as one of the great weaknesses of the European project; nothing raises more doubts about Europe, it seems, than the lack of a sense of what it means to be European.

The challenges are substantial. What can people have in common when they speak more than 60 major languages, live in a region that extends from north of the Arctic Circle to within miles of the coast of Africa, mainly know little about one another, and are divided among more than 40 different states and several hundred national groups? Bismarck once described Europe as no more than a geographical expression, and there are many today who – in the absence of compelling evidence to the contrary – still see some truth in that observation. Language is no help, because Europeans speak so many. Race is not much help either, because Caucasians are found all over the world and Europe is becoming more multiracial. Nor is religion much help, given Europe's secularism and the growth of minority (and mainly imported) religions. And for those who suggest that being European means being committed to democracy, human rights and the rule of law, none of these is a distinctly European quality.

There is also plenty of evidence to suggest that Europe is anything but a community. The member states of the EU still keep a close eye on their national interests, and the very structure of the EU institutions – made up either of national representatives or of appointees controlled by the member states – symbolizes the national mind-set of much European political thinking. And few chapters in the history of integration have reminded us so compellingly of the divisions in Europe as the euro zone crisis, which some believe will lead to the creation of a core Europe based around German leadership in the euro and a marginal group of countries that have chosen to opt out of selected joint policies. 'The dream of an expanding and more tightly integrated Greater Europe,' declared *Der Spiegel* in October 2012, 'is over.'[1]

But two critical points need to be made. First, Europeans are not alone in finding it difficult to define who they are; the same is true of Russians, Americans, the Chinese, Australians, Nigerians, and almost any other such grouping that we might care to name. Second, Europeans have not had much success in understanding what they have in common because they are reminded so often of their differences, reflected most clearly in language. It is often only when they leave Europe, mingle with the citizens of other states and look back on their homelands from afar, that they are most likely to feel European and to better appreciate the ways in which the European experience – the assumptions Europeans make, the way they see the world around them, and the way they live their lives and relate to others – is distinctive from the experience of others.

Take, for example, the role of religion. Christianity and Europe may once have been synonymous, but religion was also the source of many of Europe's most protracted and bloody conflicts, and is becoming a problem again today with the debate over Islam. Small wonder, then, that secularism has become so much a defining part of what it means to be European. While organized religion is growing almost everywhere else in the world,[2] in Europe it is shrinking, and it rarely spills over into public debates except in those few remaining states where Catholicism remains an important part of the lives of many. Even those who most vocally criticize the place of Islam in European society are doing so more on cultural than on religious grounds.

Take, also, the distinctive European approach to capital punishment. It has been outlawed in all 47 member states of the Council of Europe, and its abolition is a prerequisite for any state – such as Turkey, which complied in 2002 – that aspires to join the EU. Polls indicate that there is still some residual support for reintroducing the death penalty in parts of Europe, but there is no serious attempt so to do; its abolition is generally regarded as a *fait accompli*. And

Europeans are not stopping there; they are working also to achieve a global moratorium, and are never shy about preaching the gospel of abolition to others, or about demanding a guarantee that capital punishment is taken off the table in cases involving extradition of criminals or suspects to states that still use it.

And finally, consider the shared experiences of Europeans. Two world wars that began as European conflicts paved the way for cooperative ventures, and while the story has not always been an easy one, it is a curious aspect of human nature that shared traumas and misfortunes can be sometimes be more effective as a unifying force than successes and triumphs. The problems in the euro zone have undoubtedly been unpleasant, but no chapter in the story of the European project has been quite so effective at making us realize just how much European economies are interconnected, or has encouraged more Europeans to pay more attention to the EU.

The notion that Europeans might think along the same lines was implicit in the original arguments behind integration. Since then, the development of common policies, laws and regional institutions has helped nudge most Europeans in the same direction. Other collaborative ventures also deserve credit. Consider the Council of Europe, the European Movement and other pro-European groups, and professional associations that bring together everything from labour economists to archaeologists, cardiologists, cancer researchers and conservatoires of music; name it and there is almost sure to be a pan-European body working to promote its interests and to encourage cooperation. Shared pressures such as the cold war, internationalization and globalization have also played their role in building a European consciousness. But the work of the EU has been at the heart of it all.

To speak of European values and identities is to immediately provoke the ire of those whose chief complaint about the EU is its homogenizing effect. Polls find that while some equate 'Europe' with cultural diversity, others equate it with a loss of cultural identity. The latter celebrate and take comfort from their separate identities, which are indeed one of the great joys of Europe; the distinctive cultures, languages, architecture, art, cuisines and landscapes of the region are to be celebrated and encouraged. And yet part of the backlash against the EU is sparked by a worry that European laws and policies are undermining much of what makes the French different from the Italians and the Finns, and even what makes Walloons different from Corsicans and Sicilians.

But integration allows us to retain and protect the most important of those differences while we also enjoy the many benefits of standardization: the removal of technical barriers to trade, the guarantee of common health and safety standards, savings for businesses and consumers, and the removal of all those irritating little differences that get in the way of enjoyable international travel. Who, after all, really finds pleasure in multiple different designs for electrical outlets? The EU has given more Europeans easier access in person to other parts of Europe that once seemed exotic and distant, just as there has been a resurgence of national identity. In other words, a Spaniard can still be a Spaniard where it makes the most sense, but can also be a Catalan or a Basque or a Galician, as well as a European. These identities are not mutually exclusive, and the European project has helped remove the often parochial attitudes and hurdles that once divided Europeans, allowing the flowering of a variety of separate identities that coexist.

The EU treaties hold that 'the Community shall contribute to the flowering of the cultures of the Member States, while respecting their national and regional diversity and at the same time bringing the common heritage to the fore'. The EU motto of unity in diversity is hardly original, but it says much about the underlying character of European integration. Culture is also a facet of other EU policies, including regional and social policy, external relations, and education. In short, then, work on the development of a common European identity, and on tying down what it means to be European, has been under way for decades, and integration has helped us to see how much Europeans have in common. This has been one of the greatest unsung achievements of the European project.

The Changing Identity of Europeans

One of the criticisms levelled at the EU is that it is building a new European superstate at the expense of the individual member states. Patriots worry that they will lose what is distinctive about their home societies and that we are all moving towards a bland new Europe invented by bureaucrats, the effect being that we pay homage to invented European symbols while Brussels passes new laws that extract much that is distinctive from national cultures, piece by piece. This is certainly one of the complaints of populist and nationalist political parties such as the National Front in France, the Danish People's Party, the Dutch Party for Freedom, and the True Finns in Finland.

On the other side of the coin, there are many who argue that the idea of a European identity is an illusion, and a term that is bandied about without much sense of what it means. The term is used by critics of the EU to point out what is wrong with the European project, while supporters of the EU use it as a means of countering the argument that the EU lacks legitimacy.[3] For the novelist Umberto Eco, European identity is widespread but shallow; pride in Europe, he believes, is giving way to populism and hostility, making it all the more essential that Europeans build a more profound sense of identity.[4] There is also the broader problem of defining identity, which is more easily done at the local or national level than at the supranational level; Europe is the first phenomenon in modern history to raise the possibility that identity can be shaped at this level, which is the main reason why so many people have had such difficulty in pinning down its meaning.

It is also worth remembering that the European state is pressured at least as much from below as above. Indeed, one of the effects of integration has been to encourage more national groups within European states to push for greater self-determination and even for independence. Integration, argues Mark Leonard of the European Council on Foreign Relations, 'has lowered the stakes for separation, because the entities that emerge know they don't have to be fully autonomous and free-standing. They know they'll have access to a market of 500 million people and some of the protections of the EU'.[5]

The effects of such changes on the idea of citizenship have been profound. Being a citizen of a state means being legally associated with that state, coming under the jurisdiction of its government, having associated rights and expectations, and being treated as foreign by all other states. In addition to these legal ties, citizens are also reminded of associations with their home state by symbols and icons such as flags, anthems and leaders, and by historical figures both real and mythical. Most elementally, citizenship is about reassurance; people feel comfortable in their home environment, where everything is familiar, and when they leave that environment they begin to feel like outsiders.

Citizenship also has other benefits. It provides the kind of political and bureaucratic order that legal association brings. It has a political role in controlling the movement of people across borders, which has become increasingly urgent in the era of mass tourism, immigration, cross-border crime, international terrorism and globalization; removing too many border controls would be a recipe for chaos as economic, political and social pressures encouraged unrestricted movement from less stable and poorer states to those with more stability and opportunity. Citizenship is also a useful (if not always perfect) foundation for government and legal systems, and in deciding who has the right to vote and what they receive in return for their membership of a state.

There have been efforts to build a European citizenship for residents of the EU, but they have been insubstantial. The Treaty of Lisbon tells us that 'every person holding the nationality of a Member State shall be a citizen of the Union', but also points out that 'citizenship of the Union shall be additional to and not replace national citizenship'. All passports of EU member states issued since the mid-1980s have been printed in similar shades of burgundy and today list 'European Union' alongside the name and symbol of the member state. Legal citizens of all EU member states also have the right to move (with some conditions) to other member states, to vote and stand as candidates in local and European Parliament elections in whichever state they are legally resident, to seek the help of any EU embassy if they run into difficulties in a non-EU country where their state has no representation, to address EU institutions in any of the official languages of the EU, and to receive a reply in the same language.

These rights are pleasant enough as far as they go, but what is patently missing is the option for the citizen of an EU member state to turn in their state-issued passport and to become instead a citizen of the EU. There is a practical handicap to this: there is no European state, government or authority that would be responsible for protecting the rights of European citizens, and to which they could appeal if they ran into problems with any of the member states of the EU. Substantive EU citizenship is unlikely to be an option, then, without the creation of a European superstate. But if we think of passports as no more than handy documents that allow us to cross state borders relatively easily, and if we also consider that many of those borders in today's EU are not much more than lines on a map, then citizenship becomes as much a state of mind as a legal reality.

Consider, also, the arguments made earlier about the declining power of states, one of whose many problems is that they are often artificial in the sense that they do not coincide with the identities and interests of all those who live within their borders. For many Europeans, identification with nations is at least equally as important, if a nation is understood as a group of people who associate with one another on the basis of a shared language, ancestry, history, religion and symbols. National identity has been important to Europeans as they have worked to create their own nation-states and as minorities have sought self-determination and independence.

In some cases – Ireland and the Irish, France and the French, Portugal and the Portuguese – the lines of states and nations approximately coincide. In many other cases, though, European states are home to multiple different nationalities, and many national groups (consider Germans, Poles, Albanians and – above all – the Roma) find themselves divided among two or more states. Identity with nation has led to tensions of the kind that have been part of the conflict in Northern Ireland, were at the root of the wars in the Balkans in the 1990s, and reached their nadir with Nazism and its notions of Aryan superiority, biological racism, anti-Semitism, and the construction of a greater German empire.

Overlaying state citizenship and national identity is the idea of patriotism. At heart it means pride in country, but it can be more complicated than that: it might be value-based, meaning that a patriot believes in the merits and achievements of their home country, or it might be egocentric, meaning that a patriot loves his or her country simply because it is theirs.[6] Feelings of patriotism can be sparked by something as benign as an international football match or something as serious as a trade war or a political or military dispute with another country. It can mean non-threatening pride in a flag or a national anthem, but it has been sullied in recent decades in Europe through its co-option by right-wing nationalists beating the drum of opposition to immigration.

While states, nations, citizenship and patriotism have their place in the ordering of societies, they can also encourage a sense of superiority, exceptionalism and parochialism, and exclusive notions of keeping others out while protecting the interests of the group. Voltaire perhaps overstated it when he suggested that 'to be a good patriot one must become the enemy of the rest of mankind', but history is sprinkled with examples of the links between patriotism, violence, conflict and war. And when we hear appeals to patriotism based around defending national interests, we must ask whose interests are being defended: the people as a whole, the government of the day, or Sierra Leone, Côte d'Ivoire, and Mali who stand to benefit most from the status quo? There is also the question of why patriotism need only be based around states or nations. 'The love of one's country is a splendid thing,' suggested Pablo Casals, 'but why should love stop at the border?' Why not also (or instead) a pride in ideas? This is where Europe comes in.

Having lived for centuries with the kind of nationalist and ideological tensions that led to conflict and war, Europeans since 1945 have been less willing to lay down their lives in the interests of states or nations. This is a welcome development for which we must give at least some credit to the role of the EU in helping make internal frontiers more porous, making the rest of Europe seem less foreign (and thus less potentially threatening) to the residents of its different states and nations, helping the latter define their own interests as part of the broader European interest, and adding 'European' to the list of identities available to the people of the region.

Numerous forces and influences determine our identity, including family, community, gender, race, religion, work and language. But the further we move away from our private world, the more difficulty most of us have in explaining how we define ourselves. Family and community exert the strongest influence because they are the most real and familiar, but ask someone what it means to be Flemish, or northern Italian, or Hungarian, or Scandinavian, and the further you take them from what is most immediate and familiar, the more they will struggle to answer or to distinguish the meaning of one from the others. When it comes to being European, most will probably be tempted to associate it with the European Union, but this overlooks how far the European project has gone.

Former Czech president Václav Havel had a game stab at defining the meaning of Europe in 2000 when he described the 'basic set' of its values as including 'respect for the unique human being, and for

---

Box 8: How the EU has helped change the identity of Europeans

- It has helped Europeans better understand each other and what they have in common.
- It has changed the meaning of citizenship, which is no longer as clearly tied to states as it once was.
- It has changed the meaning of patriotism, long a source of tensions and conflict.
- Most Europeans feel some sense of identity with Europe and/or the EU.
- Europeans can choose among nations, regions, states and Europe to define themselves.
- The meaning of the term 'European' has achieved a tighter definition.

---

humanity's freedoms, rights and dignity; the principle of solidarity; the rule of law and equality before the law; the protection of minorities of all types; democratic institutions; the separation of legislative, executive and judicial powers; a pluralist political system; respect for private ownership and private enterprise, and market economy; and, a furtherance of civil society'.[7] All true enough, but these are not uniquely European beliefs, and they could all equally be claimed by an American, a Canadian, an Australian or a South Korean.

Even though critics often argue that it is hard to know what Europe represents, most of its residents have been willing to associate themselves with Europe. A survey in the EU-15 in 2004 (regrettably, not replicated since) found that about six out of ten of those asked felt some degree of association with Europe, and nearly five per cent considered themselves exclusively European (see Figure 4). A more recent survey, taken during the euro zone maelstrom in the spring of 2011 (see Figure 5), found that 62 per cent of Europeans felt they were citizens of the EU, even if – as we have seen – there is not much that constitutes European citizenship beyond a handful of rights such as free movement and the ability to vote in local and European elections. In only four EU member states – Latvia, Greece, Bulgaria and Britain – did those who felt no

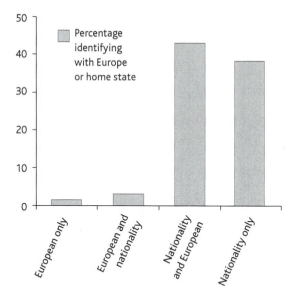

Source: European Commission, *Eurobarometer* 61 (Spring 2004), B.94.

Figure 4 Identifying with Europe

sense of citizenship with the EU outnumber those who did, and in no case was the number of 'Don't knows' more than four per cent, indicating that almost everyone has an opinion one way or the other. In short, the EU has been quite effective at promoting a sense of belonging.

The results of such surveys beg the obvious question of what makes people feel European or feel such a strong sense that they are (or are not) citizens of the EU. The simple answer is that regional integration is a shared project, based not on cooperation in the face of shared threats or fears so much as cooperation in the interests of benign and mainly beneficial economic and political goals. In their efforts to build first a single market, and then related common policies and the necessary underlying legal system, national governments have been obliged to work together, set common goals, learn more about their different situations and priorities, achieve a consensus, and – in short – identify the interests that Europeans share. The

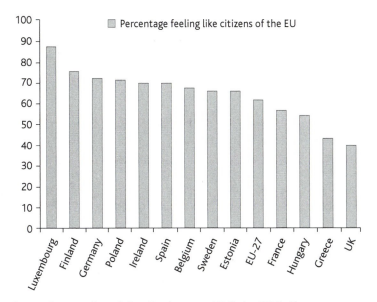

Source: European Commission, *Eurobarometer* 75 (Spring 2011), 52.

Figure 5 Citizenship of the European Union

reduction of differences has moved in parallel with a greater awareness of what makes the broad European experience distinctive from
that of people and societies in other parts of the world.

The long-term result has been the creation – argues sociologist
Neil Fligstein – of three distinctive clusters of Europeans: one made
up of about 10–15 per cent of the population that is connected by
deep economic and social ties to Europe, and benefits materially and
culturally; a second consisting of about 40–50 per cent of the population that has a more shallow relationship with Europe, aware of
what is going on across borders but still wedded to national
language, culture and politics; and a third (40–50 per cent of the
population), which tends to be older, poorer and less educated, does
not travel or consume culture from other societies, is more wedded
to home, and is more fearful of European integration.[8] The number
of people who consider themselves wholly or even mainly European
may yet be modest, but the trends are clear, and the transformation

that it represents is arguably the greatest and most lasting contribution that the work of the EU has made to the building of positive peace in the region.

The Rise of Generation E

It is hard today to remember how alien Europeans once seemed to one another. When British prime minister Neville Chamberlain described Czechoslovakia in 1938 as 'a far away country of which we know little', it was true for most Britons then, just as Britain at the time barely registered on the radar for most Czechs or Slovaks. Many Europeans still today feel a sense of distance from their neighbours, but many others – primarily the more economically and socially mobile – have exploited the new opportunities made possible by integration for unimpeded cross-border movement at greatly reduced costs. They travel as tourists, to seek new jobs, to continue their education in other countries, or to buy holiday homes or retire in other EU states with a more congenial climate or culture.

One consequence has been the rise of what has sometimes been called 'Generation E',[9] which regards internal European political borders as porous, no longer holds on to national identity in the same way as previous generations once did, and has made the most of the idea of a supranational identity. This new generation remembers home, but is at the same time acquainted with multiple countries and cultures, and perhaps even with several languages. Its members are attuned to European culture as well as to the cultures of states, regions and nations. Some of its members have become what sociologist Adrian Favell calls the 'Eurostars': those Europeans who have taken up, physically or culturally, the new opportunities for mobility offered by integration.[10]

Cultural awareness has long been part of the programme of European integration, and while there is something distasteful about culture being promoted from above rather than emerging naturally from below, the contributions of integration have been helpful. Consider the European Capital of Culture programme that has been running since 1985 under the auspices of the European Commission, which is designed to highlight the diversity of European cultures, to emphasize the cultural ties among Europeans and to foster a sense of

European citizenship. In the the face of manufacturing decline and the growth of tourism, there has been competition to win the designation, which has proved useful for the rebranding of cities as well as being a catalyst for their culture-led regeneration.[11] But success has been hard to measure, the programme is both underfunded and widely misunderstood, and cities that win the designation are often more interested in raising their profile than in wider cultural goals.[12]

Other cultural initiatives, which have similar advantages and disadvantages, include the EU Prize for Cultural Heritage designed to recognize achievements in heritage care and to showcase efforts to raise awareness about cultural heritage; the EU Prize for Contemporary Architecture aimed at recognizing modern architecture that 'is socially and culturally rooted in European cities and is important in people's everyday life'; the EU Prize for Literature (instituted in 2009) aimed at promoting greater circulation of literature and interest in non-national literary works; and European Heritage Days (co-organized by the EU and the Council of Europe) which annually open up historical buildings normally closed to the public.

Yet another is the European Heritage Label, an initiative taken by 18 European governments in 2006 that has since been adopted by the EU. Similar to the UNESCO World Heritage programme, it awards the label to sites that have had a key role in European history (as distinct from national history) as well as European integration. A related initiative is the House of European History, a project of the European Parliament intended to showcase the story of integration. Critics have cast doubt on its ability to identify a single narrative for all the member states, and have wondered how the more controversial events in European history will be interpreted. But at least it has encouraged people to think and talk about the shared European experience.

Consider also EU laws that since 1992 have better protected agricultural products and foodstuffs from defined geographical areas, giving them either protected geographical indication (PGI) or protected designation of origin (PDO) status. Thus cheeses such as gorgonzola, mozzarella, Parmigiano-Reggiano, asiago and camembert cannot be labelled as such unless they come from their home regions, the same applying to champagne, Newcastle Brown Ale, Cornish pasties, clotted cream, prosciutto and many other products.[13]

The law has been applied in the EU but is also having global effects through trade, guards the original product against inferior copies, and protects jobs in the sometimes poorer rural communities that are home to the original products. The promotion of cultural identity does not rely on cheese and champagne, to be sure, but all such steps of this kind help move us in that direction.

Nothing has been quite so central to encouraging a sense of Europeanness as education policy, where there has been a two-pronged effort to clear the way for the recognition of qualifications, and to encourage Europeans to continue their education in other countries. The EU's Erasmus programme, launched in 1987, has provided help for university exchanges and the development of multi-country degree programmes, and – for the novelist Umberto Eco – 'has created the first generation of young Europeans'.[14] More than two million students have availed themselves of the opportunity, many of them becoming bilingual or multilingual along the way, making friends and perhaps marrying across borders, and developing a heightened sense of European identity. And while this is a modest number, and fewer students have taken advantage of the exchanges than had originally been hoped (mainly because of financial and language limitations), it shows what can be done when barriers are removed and opportunities created.

As for the recognition of qualifications, making it easier for professionals to move across borders, the European Commission at first tried wading through every profession, one at a time. This generated dozens of new laws dealing with standards for everyone from doctors and nurses to lawyers and architects; it took 17 years just to negotiate the standards for architects. Then the principle of mutual recognition took hold, which says that any EU national who legally provides services in one state can do so at least temporarily or occasionally in another without having to apply for recognition of their qualifications. If they want to live and work permanently in another state, they must only show proof that their training is at a level equivalent to that required in the new state.

The Council of Europe joined the fray in 1997 with its promotion of the Lisbon Recognition Convention, an attempt to establish recognition across borders for educational qualifications. The Council had been trying since its creation in 1949 to ease the way for study abroad, developing treaties in the 1950s on the equivalence of diplomas and periods of study, but it was not until Lisbon that these efforts began to have much bite. Another Council initiative, the Bologna Accords, were signed in 1999 with the aim of creating a European higher education area within which standards and expectations for academic degrees would be comparable and compatible. Degrees had until then come in many different guises, with different names and different requirements in terms of time and content. So while a Bachelor's degree could be earned in Britain and Ireland in three years, it could take continental students as long as 5–8 years to finish, and even then there was little agreement on how to translate qualifications from one country in another.

All 47 members of the Council of Europe are now signed up to Bologna, which has established three cycles of higher education qualifications based on the European Credit Transfer and Accumulation System (ECTS), which was begun in 1992 as a pilot scheme under the Erasmus programme. The first cycle leads to a Bachelor's degree or equivalent over three years, the second to a Master's degree or equivalent over two years, and the third to a Doctoral degree over three years. And although different European countries can still use their own names for the different levels, many are switching to the Bachelors/Masters/Doctorate template. The changes have gone on to have global effects, because countries that have regular student exchanges with European countries are finding the need to work out equivalencies. The result: most of the bureaucratic hurdles that once discouraged students from studying abroad have been swept away.

Educational exchanges continue under the auspices of the EU's Lifelong Learning Programme, which promotes language learning, cross-border cooperation among schools and universities, and exchanges among students and staff. The focus has been less on Brussels and EU regulation than on encouraging coordination among the member states,[15] or – to use some unpleasant organizational jargon – the EU as a 'facilitator'. Numerous international programmes of study have since been created, and it is now easier for students and faculty to move across borders and experience different academic environments than before.

Without question, the most telling barrier to the emergence of a European identity is language: monolingualism discourages migration, reminds Europeans of their differences and foreignness, makes it more difficult for them to understand other Europeans and their cultures, and poses handicaps to businesses seeking new export markets. Language training has improved, but government policy has generally been less effective than market forces; someone wanting to improve their own professional and career prospects will be more motivated to learn another language than someone enrolled in a government scheme. English has benefited more than others; spread first by British imperialism and then by American economic and cultural power, and promoted also by its substantial and nuanced vocabulary, English is today the virtual lingua franca of Europe as well as the international language of diplomacy, commerce and entertainment, and it is hard to find many middle-class continental Europeans any more who do not have at least a basic grasp of English. The effects of this remain to be fully studied and understood.

What Do Europeans Have in Common?

What, then (to go back to the question posed at the beginning of this chapter), is a European? We cannot say that a European is a citizen of Europe, because – as we have seen – there is no such thing in strictly legal terms. So we must move on to the more complex answer: a European is someone who is a citizen of a European state and self-identifies as European in addition to, or in place of, their legal status as a citizen of their home state. As to what makes them self-identify as European, the answer lies in the values and perceptions that Europeans share. But what are these?

Among those who have attempted to answer this vexing question have been the philosophers Jürgen Habermas and Jacques Derrida. Inspired by the sight of the mass demonstrations held in multiple European cities on 15 February 2003 against the US-led invasion of Iraq, they declared the birth of a 'European public sphere', arguing that the opportunity had been created for the construction of a 'core Europe' that could offset the global influence of the United States. They listed seven qualities that they described as being part of a European 'political mentality'; these included secularization, welfarism, multilateralism, and a preference for the peaceful resolution of international problems.[16] This was an interesting first attempt, but was inadequately explained by the two authors, and did not go far enough.

Ironically, many of the most detailed and positive assessments of the European experience have come from the United States; it can sometimes seem that the number of European observers pointing out the merits of the American model (and the flaws of the European model) is approached only by the number of American observers pointing out the merits of the European model (and the flaws of the American model). The grass, it appears, continues to have a greener hue on the other side of the fence, with contrasts offered on everything from attitudes towards work and leisure to the definition of the family, the public role of the military, the priorities of education, and the principles of foreign relations. Consider these examples:

- In suggesting that the United States has placed its military and economic self-interest above goals that are in the broader global interest, Clyde Prestowitz lists what he sees as the numerous achievements of the EU, derides the short-term thinking of American policymakers, and concludes that at the heart of the difference between the two are 'the roles and responsibilities of the individual and government'. While Americans believe in equality of opportunity, he argues, Europeans have a stronger belief in equality of results.[17]
- In his controversial book *The European Dream*, Jeremy Rifkin notes the European preference for 'community relationships over individual autonomy, cultural diversity over assimilation, … sustainable development over unlimited material growth, deep play over unrelenting toil, universal human rights and the rights of nature over property rights, and global cooperation over the unilateral exercise of power'.[18]
- In *Europe's Promise*, meanwhile, Steven Hill argues that 'the European way is the best hope in an insecure age' thanks to its competitive businesses, its discovery of a means for ensuring that the benefits of capitalism are more broadly shared, its world-leading health-care systems, its inclusive democracies, and its innovative foreign policy principles.[19]

We considered two preferences at the beginning of the chapter (secularism and opposition to capital punishment) that mark out Europeans as distinctive, but there are many more.[20] Prime among them is European support for the welfare state, which has become so closely associated with Europe that it is now usual in US elections for Republican candidates to accuse their Democratic opponents of wanting to turn the United States into a 'European-style' welfare system. As *The Economist* puts it, if the United States is a defence superpower, spending almost as much on the military as the rest of the world combined, then Europe is a lifestyle superpower, spending more on social protection than the rest of the world combined.[21] While Europeans admire self-reliance, most support the idea of the government as a guarantor of societal welfare. In other words, they welcome and encourage individual endeavour, but they are also more ready than Americans to believe that the state is responsible for working to reduce economic and social differences. They are also more ready to criticize capitalism as the source of many social ills, and to believe that individual rights extend to education, health care and social security.

Second, most Europeans are instinctively communitarian. In other words, they tend to support collective ideas over individualism

---

Box 9: Ten qualities that help define what it means to be European

1. Citizenship of a European state.
2. Support for democracy, human rights and free markets.
3. Multiple identities, including national, regional, state and European.
4. Support for secularism and a distinction between church and state.
5. A preference for the welfare state and a belief that the state has a large measure of responsibility for reducing economic and social differences.
6. Support for collective ideas over individualism and self-reliance.
7. The cosmopolitan view that local and global interests cannot be separated.
8. A preference for multilateral and non-military approaches to foreign policy.
9. Pride in ideas is given priority over pride in states or nations.
10. Support for cultural diversity.

and self-reliance, preferring what the political scientist Amitai Etzioni describes as a balance 'between community and autonomy, between the common good and liberty, between individual rights and social responsibilities'.[22] Most Europeans would argue that society can sometimes be a better judge of what is good for individuals than vice versa, and that there may sometimes be good reason for the state to limit individual rights in the interests of the greater good of the community. Communitarians support the notion of positive rights, which permit or oblige action in contrast to the negative rights that do not. These attitudes help explain European support for state-subsidized education and housing, a safe environment and universal health care.

Third, most Europeans show a distinctively cosmopolitan bent in their view of the world, meaning that they take the view that all humans belong to a single community, that local and global interests and concerns cannot be separated or divorced, and that the world is ultimately the only community that matters. Cosmopolitan ideas are at the heart of the Universal Declaration of Human Rights and its focus on rights as the entitlement of all, regardless of race, gender, religion, national or social origin, or the political, jurisdictional or international status of the country or territory to which people belong. Cosmopolitan ideas are also at the heart of European integration, promoted by the removal of the economic, legal, political and even psychological barriers that for so long encouraged Europeans to place state and nation above the idea of belonging to a wider community of human experience. They also help us understand the European preferences for civilian power and multilateral approaches to foreign policy (discussed in more detail in Chapter 7). In short, integration has meant the replacement of the exclusionary ideas associated with states and nations by the more inclusionary ideas related to Europe as a whole. As the German sociologist Ulrich Beck puts it, if nationalism is based on the principle of 'either/or', then cosmopolitanism is based on the principle of 'both/and'.[23]

Fourth, Europeans tend to be sympathetic to the idea of constitutional patriotism. This is an academic idea that draws less attention than it deserves, describing a belief that the universal principles of the democratic constitutional state are the only acceptable basis for identification with a state.[24] In other words, pride in the ideas on which liberal constitutions are based is preferable to pride in states themselves. The idea traces its roots to post-war West Germany, which was grappling with the challenge of trying to rediscover pride in itself without reverting to the kind of nationalism that had spawned Hitler. As nationalism and identity with states have lost their lustre, Europeans have come to identify more with the broader ideas that they all support, including democracy, human rights and the rule of law. They still take pride in states and feel comfortable in what they represent, but most shy away from the exclusionist and chauvinist ideas that come with that pride.

Fifth, Europeans have an instinctive sympathy with (and a long tradition of) multiculturalism. It may seem daring to suggest this so soon after so many European leaders (including Angela Merkel and David Cameron) have declared the death and/or failure of multiculturalism in Europe, but a closer reading of their statements reveals that they have used the term as a convenient code for their concerns about the future of racial and religious tolerance in Europe. Too fearful of suggesting that multiracialism or religious tolerance in Europe is dead, they have instead opted for the softer idea that tolerance of other cultures is in trouble. In truth, not only is multiculturalism alive and well in the region, but it has long been at the heart of the European experience: complex patterns of immigration and invasion dating back centuries have exposed Europeans to different cultures, and they have routinely adopted and integrated values from the new groups with which they have come into contact.

To conclude, then: Bismarck's idea that Europe is no more than a geographical expression long ago lost its relevance, and Geremek's concerns about the creation of Europeans are less real than many might suppose. The differences among Europeans are reflected in the existence of multiple languages, states and nations, but closer examination reveals patterns of behaviour, shared values and common experiences that among them constitute the ingredients of a community of Europeans. While the debate about Europe has been focused on the work of the EU and other bodies, it seems that Europeans have followed their own trajectory towards building a sense of shared purpose. The ingredients were almost certainly there before the construction of what later became the European Union, but the EU has played a major role in encouraging this new kind of thinking and in helping Europeans remember and value what unites them over what divides them.

Europe as a Political Model

We have seen how the charges of the eurosceptics are out of step with the thinking of the majority of Europeans. Polls reveal that, by large majorities, Europeans support the EU and consider it to be both democratic and modern (even if enthusiasm has tailed off in the wake of the euro zone crisis). Polls also reveal that more people trust the EU institutions than trust their own national governments. On only one major issue is euroscepticism more closely aligned with public opinion: the European institutions are widely considered to be inefficient.[1]

But while the EU institutions are certainly imperfect, so are all large organizations or networks of institutions, whether local or national, private or public in their reach. Who among us, after all, does not have unhappy stories to tell about dealing with bureaucracies or of trying to find our way to a responsive (even, sometimes, a human) corporate customer service agent?

It is a curious aspect of the debate about Europe that the EU institutions are criticized for their flaws as though they were almost unique in having such flaws. They are, for example, derided for being a source of questionable new regulations as though European lawmakers had mastered a skill that has so far eluded lawmakers at the national and local level. The decision-making procedures of the EU institutions are censured for being slow and cumbersome as though national procedures were conspicuously swift and efficient. And the EU is regularly denounced for its inability to provide leadership in times of need as though national political leaders had superior skills in this regard. In commenting on the October 2012 EU summit, the BBC's Europe editor, Gavin Hewitt, noted that 'compromising and fudging is the way business often gets done in Brussels'.[2] But this is also the way it gets done in most national democracies.

European integration has certainly had its share of institutional problems, but this should not blind us to how much the European model has to offer as a model for making decisions and doing political business. It still makes sense for individual states to make their own decisions on a host of policy matters, but the pressures of globalization and freer trade have combined with the need for countries to work together on shared or common problems to give new value to the kinds of cooperative decision-making skills in which the EU has become the clear global leader. Integration has encouraged Europeans to take a broader view of problems and their solutions, promoting compromise and consensus decision making rather than the often self-interested and narrow perspective of states. Integration has also gone beyond mere cooperation by allowing Europeans to draw from a wider and deeper pool of ideas and expertise, as well as encouraging them to be more ambitious in the standards and targets they set, bringing the laggards up to higher levels of achievement rather than allowing them to act as a drag on efforts to resolve pressing problems, and creating additional levels of protection that national governments working alone might have been more reluctant to provide.

Ironically, some of the clearest benefits of the EU approach can be found in one area where the EU is usually subject to its most sustained criticism: the laws that it adopts. It is near impossible to know how many EU laws are operative at any given time, or the proportion of national laws that stem from the requirements of EU law, but eurosceptics have exploited the uncertainties to sustain the myth that the EU has been the source of large numbers of burdensome and occasionally absurd new laws, and that the number of national laws arising out of EU requirements has snowballed. In reality, the number of active EU laws is greatly outnumbered by the number of active national and local laws, and EU law has brought with it considerable qualitative benefits: it has often resulted in the abolition of inefficient national laws, and it has often made life easier for European business while providing increased protection for European consumers.

It is also ironic that while one school of critics regrets the growing volume of EU laws, another argues that there are not enough. There are still many areas of business activity, for example, that could benefit from EU laws designed to remove national barriers. There are also many examples of EU policy that are deservedly castigated for being inefficient and in need of reform (agricultural and fisheries policy comes most readily to mind), and yet where the answer lies at least in part in the agreement of new laws, or certainly the replacement of old ones with new ones.

And if critics remain unconvinced, they have only to consider the multiple examples of regional integration around the world to realize that many others seem to agree that Europe may be on to something. There is now almost no part of the world that is not involved in efforts to promote regional integration in one form or another, or that has not signed free trade agreements with others. They may not have followed the European exemplar in every detail; many have been as interested in Europe's mistakes as in its achievements, and the prospects for the success of these different initiatives are variable. But by virtue of being the biggest and the oldest example of regional integration in the modern era, it is to the European model that most of the others have looked for reference, whether as a guide or a warning.

The Advantages of the European Approach

We saw earlier that the modern state is rife with problems. States impose artificial divisions on human society, they encourage people to think in sectional and self-interested terms, they impede free movement, their record of policy effectiveness has been mixed, they have an unfortunate habit of bickering and going to war with one another, and they often oblige diverse groups of people to live against their will under a common system of government. In short, the state is an imperfect model, and even with more than 300 years of experience has been unable to work out many of the kinks in its system.

One answer to the problems of states is for them to break down into smaller units. This was a phenomenon that we saw in Europe in the nineteenth century as nationalists struggled to free themselves from the control of empires, and that we see again in Europe today as nationalists campaign for greater self-determination and cultural recognition: the powers of national governments in Spain, Belgium, France, Britain and other countries are accordingly being devolved to local communities. But while this fragmentation brings government closer to the governed, its also runs the danger of encouraging interests to be defined more narrowly, increases the number of political and legal jurisdictions and the number of interested parties that must sit around the negotiating table to address shared problems, and potentially reduces the chances of reaching agreement. Far better to devolve to local units the matters best addressed by them, while also working together at the regional and European level to address shared problems (a concept known as subsidiarity).

The core benefit of regional integration is that it both devolves and combines decision making, retaining the best of what the state has to offer while addressing many of its flaws. Thus integration has encouraged Europeans to take a broader view of the needs and problems of the societies in which they live, and to work together on shared and common problems. Take the example of environmental policy, where the efficient management of air, water and other shared resources is more likely to be achieved through cross-border cooperation. But that we have made so little progress in addressing the problem of climate change reflects how much we are still held hostage to states pursuing self-interest. The science is clear, damage is obviously being done, we have a good idea what to expect without remedial action, and we have a good idea about what needs to be done to fix the problem. And yet states continue to defend their narrow interests at the expense of the broader good. There is more chance of progress on this and similar problems if the discussions are conducted not among self-interested and competitive governments, but instead through cooperative ventures such as the European Union.

A second advantage of the European project lies in its capacity to promote compromise and consensus decision making. Where states, regions and nations focus on what is in their own interest, making policy at the European level involves more people and interests in a decision, takes into account a greater variety of opinions and agendas, encourages cooperation among like-minded groups in multiple countries, and moves us away from the habit of zero-sum games involving winners and losers. Building a consensus can be frustrating, because it demands more time and thought. It also often fails in its intent, the inability of governments to agree on how to respond to the euro zone crisis being a particularly large and obvious case in point. But consensus is also the essence of democracy. As Abraham Lincoln might have said, some of us can have our own way all of the time, and all of us can have our own way some of the time, but none of us can have our own way all of the time.

Third, integration allows Europeans to draw from a wider and deeper pool of resources, talent and ideas. While states draw mainly on expertise and resources within their borders, offering them fewer opportunities to learn from the achievements and mistakes of others, the European project promotes learning by the sharing of ideas and the comparison of approaches and outcomes. While many worry (and not entirely without cause) that the options of the individual member states of the EU are being restrained by the need to take into consideration a wider set of interests, we should also remember that the perspectives of others have often made our lives better.

Consider the access to resources offered by the EU's cohesion policy, which channels investments to the poorer parts of the EU. The domestic efforts of member states have their part to play in redistribution and levelling the playing field, but they can only go so far. By taking a multi-state approach, EU policy sets more standardized goals, helps reduce overlap and duplication, taps into more funds and opportunities, helps create new jobs and wealthier consumers, and in turn helps raise standards across a wider geographical area, thereby making the EU more globally competitive. In the budgetary period 2007–13, about €350 billion was earmarked for regional spending, adding to the enormous amounts already spent since the first grants were made to depressed industrial areas by the European Coal and Steel Community in the 1950s. Cohesion policy has been criticized for its lack of clear goals, its failure to set priorities, and problems with monitoring how funds have been used,[3] but few would suggest that the answer is to abandon the policy so much as to make it more efficient and effective.

Fourth, integration has encouraged Europeans to raise targets and standards through the pressures of the leader–laggard dynamic through which laws and regulations are harmonized at the level of progressive states. For example, many poorer EU member states – such as Greece, Portugal and Romania – had little in the way of environmental standards in place when they first joined. This stood in contrast to the more progressive policies and laws adopted by Germany, the Netherlands and the Scandinavian states. With the need to remove barriers to the single market, and the obligations on new member states to adopt existing EU law and policy, the laggard states have been compelled to meet higher targets on air and water quality, the management of chemicals, waste control, energy efficiency,

---

Box 10: Six advantages of thinking like a European

1. Encourages a broader view of societal problems and needs.
2. Promotes compromise and consensus decision making.
3. Allows decision-makers to draw from a wider and deeper pool of resources, talent and ideas.
4. Encourages more ambitious targets and the raising of standards.
5. Generates laws and policies that offer higher levels of protection.
6. Promotes efficiency and the more effective resolution of shared or common problems.

---

control of pesticides and the protection of biodiversity. Had they maintained different standards, market pressures would have made products and services from cleaner states more expensive (because of the costs of higher standards) and encouraged companies in those states to move jobs to states with weaker regulations. As it is, the tension between the leaders and laggards has encouraged a rise to higher standards rather than a decline to the lowest common denominator.

Finally, integration has resulted in peer and market pressures that have led to the joint development of laws and policies giving additional levels of protection that national governments working alone might have been unable or more reluctant to provide. Consider these examples:

- Food safety standards have improved, including a ban on hormone-treated beef, the control of excessive nutritional and health claims by producers, and improved labelling requirements for ingredients, calories, and sugar, fat and salt content.
- A decade-long struggle led to the passage in 1985 of an EU law making manufacturers liable for harm or loss due to defective products; EU laws have strengthened the rights of consumers to returns and refunds and to fair and transparent contracts; and the protection of personal data has been strengthened since the passage of a 1995 EU law.
- Health is better protected by laws setting common standards for pesticide residue levels in food, requiring that all toys sold in the

EU must meet the same safety standards (notably on chemicals, heavy metals and allergens), and setting common quality and safety standards for human blood and blood components in order to help prevent the transmission of diseases.

- EU law prohibits the testing of cosmetics on animals, has established limits on animal testing on laboratories, and sets standards for the treatment of farm animals. An Animal Welfare Strategy was launched in 2012, aimed at improving compliance with EU law, simplifying the rules and bureaucratic procedures, and filling gaps in the law.
- Common standards on working conditions and employment benefits mean that every EU citizen, regardless of the member state in which they live and work, has the same number of working hours and days, the same workplace safety conditions, the same rights to paid holidays, and the same protection against discrimination.

There have also been positive spin-offs in the area of police and judicial cooperation. The need for EU states to work together on immigration and cross-border crime has resulted in efforts to standardize the processing of applications for asylum, to manage immigration by skilled workers while also controlling illegal immigration (an EU blue card was adopted in 2009 in order to standardize conditions and rights of residence for highly qualified non-EU nationals, albeit with restricted terms), to develop policies on visas and personal data protection, to establish common rules on the provision of legal aid, and to encourage cooperation among police forces and judicial authorities. The single market would have faced greater resistance without the assurances offered by enhanced public security, and more troubling questions would have been raised about enlargement.

Since the launch in 1995 of passport-free travel in the Schengen area, the Schengen Information System has simplified the exchange of information designed to control the movement of criminals across borders, and has broadcast alerts concerning missing people and property. Since 1999, Europol has helped national police forces cooperate in addressing threats that are notoriously difficult for individual states to tackle alone, including terrorism, organized crime, cyber crime, clandestine immigration networks, money forging and laundering, and the trafficking of drugs, vehicles, people, child pornography and radioactive materials. It was joined in 2002 by Eurojust, which has improved investigations and criminal prosecutions involving two or more member states. European arrest and evidence warrants have been agreed, the former replacing the lengthy extradition process once involved in European cross-border criminal actions, and the latter standardizing methods for obtaining evidence in cross-border cases. Consider these examples of the resulting successes:

- Operations carried out in cooperation with Europol during 2012 resulted in the breaking up of an operation involving Greek and Bulgarian criminals who were counterfeiting euro coins, the closing of a Colombian print-shop producing counterfeit banknotes in euros, US dollars and British pounds, and the disruption of a Romanian-based group involved in credit card fraud and illegal online purchases.
- An investigation begun in 2010 and involving Belgium, Bulgaria, France and Poland resulted in 2012 in the breaking up of a network trafficking young women from Bulgaria for sexual exploitation. Earlier operations dismantled a group bringing illegal Filipino migrants to Denmark and France, and another based in Hungary that was smuggling illegal immigrants from the Middle East to Austria and Germany.
- In 2010, police forces in Austria, Belgium, France, Italy, Lithuania and Sweden worked together with the help of Europol to identify and arrest members of separate criminal groups involved in a series of ram-raids in several continental EU states, where gangs crashed stolen vehicles into the entrances of electrical retailers, bagging as many high-value products as they could before quickly dispersing.
- Also in 2010, an operation codenamed Diabolo II and involving Europol, Interpol and police forces in 13 Asian and 27 European countries led to the seizure of more than 65 million counterfeit cigarettes and nearly 400,000 other counterfeit items – including cameras, toys, shoes, hats and handbags bearing more than 20 different trademarks – brought to Europe from Asia in shipping containers.

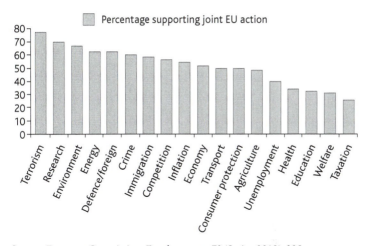

Source: European Commission, *Eurobarometer* 73 (Spring 2010), 205.

Figure 6   Support for joint EU policymaking

The advantages of the EU model have struck a note with most Europeans, who support joint decision making in a wide range of policy areas (see Figure 6). Terrorism has moved to the top of that list in the last decade, followed by scientific research and development, and by joint approaches to the environment and energy policy. There is also majority support for a combined EU approach to foreign and defence policy, which is surprising considering how slow the progress has been on both fronts. Less remarkable are the lower levels of support for joint decision making on health, education, welfare and tax policy, all still the preserves of the member states, and proof of the many areas in which the authority of those states has been retained even after decades of integration.

Few if any of these advantages would have existed without the European Union, and they would almost all stand to be lost to a member state that was to leave the EU. Individual states can cooperate without the help of an integrative body such as the EU, but they are more interested in national than in shared or joint interests, the chances of successfully resolving problems are diminished, and the formal agreements they reach are usually looser, more numerous, and less easily monitored or enforced. They can still learn from one another, and draw on their separate pools of talent, but they see themselves more as competitors than as collaborators, and will always be obliged to keep a closer eye on other states to ensure that they are respecting their agreements. And the motivation to raise targets and standards, and to agree common policies, will always be greatly diminished without the heightened sense of cooperation that the EU has been so adept at promoting.

The European Union as a Lawmaker

No discussion of the qualities of the EU as a model for doing political business would be complete without addressing the hoary complaint that it is a source of burdensome laws and regulations. To hear its work described, we might be forgiven for believing that the European Quarter in Brussels was populated by humourless Eurocrats hatching devious plans for onerous and occasionally absurd new rules designed to limit the choices of hapless Europeans and to eat away at the distinctive personalities of the member states of the EU. Certainly this is the conclusion of the indefatigably eurosceptic British commentator Christopher Booker, who has identified in EU law entirely spurious threats to everything from double-decker buses to oak trees, Scotch whisky, cheddar cheese and Cox's Orange Pippin apples. In a final flourish of folly, he describes this problem as 'the new totalitarianism'.[4]

Leaving aside the absurdity of likening the European Union to North Korea, it is impossible to be sure of the precise size of the EU 'burden', because it is difficult to be sure exactly how many EU laws are active at any given time, a problem that applies also at the national and local levels. And even if we could, not all laws are equal in regard to how many people they affect or how much they cost. The EU institutions themselves generate legally binding acts such as regulations and directives, but many of them set general goals rather than specific obligations, others amend or fine-tune older laws, and yet others are both narrow and highly technical in their objectives. Consider, for example, a one-page regulation from May 2012 that suspends import duties on industrial sugar for one year, or a 2011 regulation that lays down rules for the implementation of an earlier regulation on the collection, transmission and processing of statistical data on education and training systems. To give these the same weight and value as, for example, the 2003 directive setting up a greenhouse gas emission allowance trading scheme or the 2005 directive on the recognition of professional qualifications is absurd.

Eurosceptics like to quote the 1988 prediction by Commission president Jacques Delors that within a decade, as much as 80 per cent of economic law, and perhaps also of fiscal and social law, would be of European origin.[5] But they also neglect to point out that this came nowhere close to happening, and the myth of a European lawmaking factory has since been widely adopted, as illustrated by just one small example of a difference in calculations. In 2010, the European Commission claimed that there were about 8400 regulations and nearly 2000 directives in force in the EU,[6] a figure that was accepted by Open Europe, a London-based think-tank on European reform. Adding in decisions (which have narrow and specific targets, and administrative rather than legislative goals) and miscellaneous other acts takes the total to just short of 26,000.[7] But a eurosceptic former MEP from Denmark named Jens-Peter Bonde has estimated the number of pieces of 'valid law decided in the European institutions' at just under 29,400, and by adding in standards, international agreements, and verdicts of the Court of Justice, has pushed the total number of binding acts to which EU citizens are subject to the entirely misleading total of just over 103,000.[8]

A more neutral and considered source was a 2010 research paper published by the British House of Commons Library, which began by pointing out that being sure of the number of active EU laws was difficult, for several reasons:

- EU and national databases are not always reliable.
- Few of the electronic databases used to trace EU legislation predate the early 1990s.
- Differentiating between EU-generated and nationally generated changes to the law is not easy.
- The proportion of EU-based national law varies from year to year.
- There is little data on the relative material impact of EU and national laws.
- EU regulations are not usually transposed into national legislation so much as into quasi-legislative measures that do not pass through a national parliamentary process.

- EU regulations have different levels of impact from one member state to another.
- EU law is transposed and implemented differently, some member states implementing several EU laws in one omnibus instrument while others implement laws individually.[9]
- EU laws come and go; an average of nearly 900 EU laws expired or were repealed annually between 1997 and 2009.[10]

We should also remember that since so much EU law is designed to harmonize existing practice, the growth in the number of EU laws has led to a concomitant decrease in the number of separate and competing national laws, leaving Europeans overall subject to fewer obligations, or at the very least to more standardized obligations. Consider the abolition of the fuss that once accompanied travel across internal borders in the EU: gone for the most part are the days of visas and long queues at immigration – the crossing of most international borders within the EU instead often happens quite literally in the blink of an eye. Consider also the General Safety Regulation of 2009, which required a basket of new safety features in road vehicles and replaced more than 50 existing directives.

Consider also the example of patent law. It costs Europeans up to five times as much as Americans to register patents because they are obliged to lodge applications and seek validation in multiple countries and languages, a situation that interferes with innovation and improved European competitiveness. Efforts to agree a European approach were long delayed by the desire of different countries to have their languages recognized, but with an agreement reached in 2011 by 25 of the 27 countries (the hold-outs being Italy and Spain), patents will now be valid once granted by the European Patent Office in English, French and German only. The brushing aside of a tangle of conflicting national laws has made life easier for Europe's inventors.

Consider these other examples of the regulatory burden being reduced by EU law:

- The European statute that allows companies incorporated in different member states to merge or form a holding company or joint subsidiary without the need to meet different sets of national legal requirements.

- Changes that have created a single set of standards for the release of new medicinal products onto the EU market, replacing the separate authorizations that companies were once obliged to win in each member state.
- EU laws dating back to the early 1960s that have resulted in a single harmonized system of E-numbers for listing food additives such as colourings, preservatives, sweeteners, antioxidants, stabilizers and thickeners.

Even the common eurosceptic charge that laws are made in Brussels is misleading, because – and this is a point worth repeating since it is a mistake made even by many of the academic experts on the EU – 'Brussels' does not have independent powers to enact laws. As we saw in Chapter 1, there are numerous limits on the Commission in regard to the areas in which it can propose new laws, and the decisions on which proposals for new EU laws will or will not be enacted are taken by a combination of the directly elected European Parliament and the Council of the EU, which consists of government ministers from the member states working alongside the Brussels-based permanent representatives of the member states. In other words, the laws that come from 'Brussels' actually come from agreements thrashed out by institutions representing the interests of European voters or staffed by government officials from the member states. That there is some independently functioning community of lawmakers in Brussels is pure fiction.

Box 11: Six misconceptions about European law

1. The body of active EU laws is substantial.
2. Most national laws are generated by the requirements of EU law.
3. EU law has led to an increased regulatory burden on consumers and business.
4. EU law has undermined and undercut the distinctive personalities of EU member states.
5. 'Brussels' has independent powers to make laws, and national lawmakers are losing much of their authority.
6. Many of the goals of EU law are petty and eccentric.

One person who has failed to understand – or perhaps to *want* to understand – the powers of EU institutions is Douglas Carswell, a eurosceptic Conservative member of the British Parliament. Responding to the House of Commons Library report, he argued that it 'clearly shows the extent to which public policy is now made by EU institutions and British ministers are left to pretend that they are making the decisions … Very many regulations now come from Europe and there's very little those we elect at the ballot box can do about it'.[11] But ministers *do* make the decisions (working with their counterparts from the other member states), voters have direct representation in the decision-making process through their Members of the European Parliament (as well as indirect representation through their elected national legislators), the treaties guide and limit the EU lawmaking process, and almost anyone can challenge the legitimacy of EU laws by taking a case to the European Court of Justice if they feel that boundaries have been overstepped.

The difficulty of determining the exact size of the body of EU law means that it is also difficult to compare the volumes of EU-generated and nationally generated law, and the UK is again an instructive example. The government maintains a web site that lists laws enacted and revised since 1267,[12] which sounds impressive until we realize that it contains no complete annual data sets prior to the late 1980s. Since then, the number of new statutory instruments adopted annually for the UK has ranged from a low of 1468 in 1987 to a high of 3133 in 2011, working out to an average of roughly 2000 per year. To this must be added public general acts, local acts, and acts of the Scottish, Welsh and Northern Irish regional assemblies. But this is still no more than a count of the number of instruments adopted each year, which does not tell us how many are active at any given time, or anything about the breadth and depth of their effects.

The same problem pertains to all other EU member states, but this has not stopped critics from engaging in creative but mainly wrongheaded speculation. The extent of the uncertainty is reflected in the range of estimates, which suggest that anything from six per cent to 84 per cent of national laws trace their origins to EU law. Unsurprisingly, eurosceptics opt for the higher numbers in their efforts to convince Europeans of their loss of sovereignty, but the story about the origins of that 84 per cent figure illustrates the flawed logic that is often brought to bear on the matter. It comes from a reply given to a question in the German Bundestag in 2005, which suggested that in the period 1998–2004, nearly 19,000 EU directives and regulations had been adopted in Germany as compared to about 3500 federal laws. This was taken up by former German president Roman Herzog, and later adopted by eurosceptic politicians in other countries.[13]

But the German figure excluded the number of laws passed at the *Länder* and local level in Germany (which is, after all, a federal state), and made no allowance for the breadth or depth of the laws passed. Many EU laws, as noted earlier, are both focused and technical, while many national laws are only partially the result of EU obligations. It is also likely that some of the national laws arising out of European law would have been adopted even without the EU, because Germany would still have had an interest in removing barriers to trade, and in protecting its businesses and consumers. Furthermore, the figure quoted does not take into account those instances where EU law replaced or rationalized pre-existing national laws. And finally, the effects of EU law vary from one member state to another, having their greatest reach in those southern and eastern member states that have had to make the greatest efforts to meet the terms of EU membership; housecleaning in the wake of the end of communism, for example, meant much greater adjustments for countries such as Bulgaria and Romania.

Returning to the more objective assessment of the House of Commons Library report, it warns that in the British case 'there is no totally accurate, rational or useful way of calculating the percentage of national laws based on or influenced by the EU'. It is able to conclude only that between 1997 and 2009, just under seven per cent of primary legislation in the UK and just over 14 per cent of secondary legislation could be tied to the obligations of implementing EU rules, while also noting that 'the degree of involvement varied from passing reference to explicit implementation'. However, reflecting the often selective manner in which numbers are quoted to suit the case being made, the eurosceptic British newspaper the *Telegraph* ran a story on the Commons report under the headline 'Up to half of British laws come from Europe, House of Commons Library claims'. This might have been true in some years, but as a general conclusion it was patently misleading.

Critics of the EU also like to poke fun at some of the more risible examples of EU law, the perennial favourite being a 1989 rule that classified fruit and vegetables in part by their appearance. The well-intentioned idea behind this law was to help consumers better compare products across state lines, and the criteria used included the curvature of cucumbers and the smoothness of carrots. The notion begged to be mocked, but it also raised more general concerns about the utility of law, and political pressure led to an amendment that lifted the visual appearance requirements from all but the ten biggest-selling fruits and vegetables (including apples, oranges, lettuce and tomatoes), while member states were allowed to sell less comely products under a special label. The many examples of questionable EU laws have helped sustain a cottage industry of speculation about entirely mythical laws, including those requiring circus tightrope walkers to wear hard hats, lorry drivers to eat healthier breakfasts, and barmaids to cover their cleavages.

Once again, to suggest that EU lawmakers have unique skills in the art of the bizarre is to overlook the long history of peculiar lawmaking at the national level. To be fair, many of the rules still on the statute books in European states are the often-forgotten and no-longer-enforced heritage of legislative initiatives taken hundreds of years ago. Thus in Britain it is still illegal to die in the Houses of Parliament, it remains legal to kill a Scotsman within the city walls of York if he is carrying a bow and arrow, and it is considered treason to place a postage stamp bearing the head of the monarch upside-down on an envelope.[14] More contemporary examples include a British law requiring householders to nominate a neighbour to turn off their alarm while they are away,[15] a Swiss law that forbids men from relieving themselves standing up after 10 pm, a French law against naming pigs Napoleon,[16] and a law that came into effect in 2013 in the US state of Kansas limiting pet owners to no more than four cats per household. The examples go on, but the point remains: to single out the EU as a source of questionable laws is to ignore the bigger picture.

Europe as an Example

If imitation is the sincerest form of flattery, then the EU can consider itself flattered, because there are today few parts of the world that are not engaged in some form of exercise in regional integration or – at the very least – free trade. Some countries are members of not just one but two and sometimes even three different regional associations, and when the African Union was created in 2001 it was an almost direct copy of the European model, with a Commission, a Parliament, a Court of Justice, an Assembly based on the European Council, an investment bank and a central bank. Conversely, it is hard to find countries that have entirely abstained from regional integration; they tend to be troubled or pariah states such as North Korea and Cuba, or disputed territories such as Western Sahara and Palestine.

The motives for setting up regional groupings are varied, as are their chances of success, and it is quite possible that regional integration would have happened even without the European example. And it would be wrong to imply that other exercises in integration have directly copied the European model; some have followed the EU into economic cooperation, a customs union, free trade and monetary union, while others have a more ambiguous interest in cooperation, and the mistakes made by Europe have taught them as much as have its successes.

The prospects of viable integration also vary according to what the political scientist Joseph Nye has described as integrative potential, or the conditions needed to achieve successful integration. These include the economic equality and compatibility of the states involved, the extent to which elites in the participating states think alike on economic policy, and the capacity of those states to adapt and respond to public demands, which in turn depends on the stability and responsiveness of government.[17] Thus while the African Union is undoubtedly ambitious, with 54 members covering almost the entire continent of Africa, the political instability, poverty and social divisions of many of its member states leave it with numerous obstacles to overcome.

But Europe was the clear modern pioneer of regional integration on a wide scale. The European Coal and Steel Community was created by the 1951 Treaty of Paris, opened for business in August 1952, and was followed in 1958 by the European Economic Community and in 1960 by the European Free Trade Association. (The Council of Europe was founded in 1949 but is less interested in integration than in cooperation.) Elsewhere, the Council of Arab Economic Unity was founded in 1957, and the 1960s saw the creation of the Latin American Free Trade Association, the Economic Community of Central African States, the Association of Southeast Asian Nations, and the Andean Community. Some of the early experiments have fallen by the wayside, some have changed their goals and names, others have evolved into new organizations, and yet others have been transformed from modest exercises in cooperation into more ambitious efforts to encourage regional cooperation (see Table 2).

Table 2   Regional integration around the world

Region	Name	Date of origin or founding	Number of members
Europe	European Union	1951	28
	European Free Trade Association	1960	4
North America	North American Free Trade Agreement	1994	3
South America	Central American Integration System	1960	7
	Andean Community	1969	4
	Latin American Integration Association	1960	14
	Southern Common Market (Mercosur)	1991	4
	Union of South American Nations (combining the Andean Community and Mercosur)	2008	12
Caribbean	Caribbean Community	1973	15
Pacific Rim	Asia Pacific Economic Cooperation	1989	21
Asia	Association of Southeast Asian Nations	1967	10
	South Asian Association for Regional Cooperation	1985	8
	Eurasian Economic Community	2000	6
Middle East	Council of Arab Economic Unity	1957	18
	Gulf Cooperation Council	1981	6
Africa	East African Community	1967–77, 2000–	5
	Economic Community of West African States	1975	15
	Economic Community of Central African States	1966	10
	Southern African Development Community	1980	15
	African Union	2001	54

One of the more successful is the Association of Southeast Asian Nations (ASEAN), founded in 1967 with a looser institutional system than the EU, and including among its members such regional economic powerhouses as Indonesia, Malaysia, the Philippines and Singapore. From an initial interest in security issues, ASEAN's priorities expanded to include economic cooperation and trade. Its members agreed in 1992 to create a free trade area (on slightly different terms from the EU), and in 2010 signed a free trade agreement with China – the largest such agreement in the world by population, and the third largest by GDP. The proposed next step is an ASEAN+3 agreement that would bring ASEAN, China, Japan and South Korea into an East Asian free trade area. There have been problems of late sparked by China's claims over islands and territorial waters in the South China Sea, and worries about China's growing power and belligerence (too much political and economic asymmetry has always been a threat to regional integration), but troubles are always to be expected, as the EU case has shown.

Similar problems (and possibilities) are posed further west by the role of India in the eight-member South Asian Association for Regional Cooperation (SAARC), founded in 1985. Its governments have agreed to promote 'collective self-reliance' in 16 policy areas, including agriculture, transport and telecommunications, and its leaders meet at annual summits rotating among the different countries. Its goals are modest compared to those of the EU, its interests being primarily with free trade, and its biggest problem is the enormous size of India, which accounts for more than two-thirds of the population of the SAARC and nearly 40 per cent of its GDP. It has deliberately turned a blind eye to problems between its member states, such as the Indo-Pakistan dispute over Kashmir, and is handicapped by the severe political difficulties of members such as Afghanistan and Pakistan.

Latin America has also been interested in regional integration, its earliest experiments focused first on Central America and then on the Andean region. The Latin American Free Trade Association was launched in 1960, but a combination of overly ambitious goals and authoritarian politics in several member states derailed the process. Chile and Peru set up the separate Andean Group in 1969, which was followed in 1991 by the Southern Common Market, or Mercosur, based around Argentina and Brazil. The 12 members of

these two groups subsequently decided to explore closer cooperation, leading to the creation in 2008 of the Union of South American
Nations (UNASUR). It has institutions that look much like those of
the EEC in its early days, and is working on the construction of a
single market and cooperation in a number of policy fields, including
immigration and security.

For their part, North Americans have had less success with integration. A 1989 US–Canadian free trade agreement evolved with the
addition of Mexico in 1992 into the North American Free Trade
Agreement (NAFTA), with the modest goals of phasing out tariffs on
selected products, phasing out of barriers to agricultural trade, opening up the North American advertising market, and loosening rules
on the movement of corporate executives and some professionals.
But NAFTA is handicapped by the economic differentials between
Mexico and its two partners, the hostility of US labour unions, the
implications for immigration from Mexico, concerns among environmentalists about the weaker standards south of the Rio Grande,
and – particularly since 9/11 and in the wake of the Mexican drug
war – worries about security.

Africa's experience with integration, meanwhile, has been mixed.
If the African Union faces an uphill struggle, the continent has several
more regionally focused organizations with smaller memberships and
better chances of success. The three-member East African
Community was founded in 1967 with the in-built advantages of a
common currency, a customs union, a lingua franca (English), and a
shared transport system. But it broke up in acrimony in 1977 when it
became clear to Uganda and Tanzania that Kenya was reaping most
of the rewards. It was relaunched in 2000, Rwanda and Burundi
joined the club, and the new iteration set itself the goals of a single
market, a single currency, and even – by 2015 – political federation.

Further west, the 16-member Economic Community of West
African States (ECOWAS) set out in 1975 to achieve first a customs
union and then a full common market along the lines of the EU. But
while several of its members (notably Ghana and Senegal) are relatively stable, several others (such as Burkina Faso, Liberia and Sierra
Leone) are not, and the smaller members cast worried eyes at
Nigeria, which has more than half the population of ECOWAS and
is by far its largest, wealthiest and most powerful partner.
Conversely, some Nigerians resent the extent to which their country

has borne much of the financial burden of ECOWAS. And yet Nigeria could provide leadership and economic opportunities, and in return promote peace and access to new markets, by investing in its poorer neighbours.

These and other examples show that regional integration has a broader historical significance: it is the logical effect of the long-term trend towards international cooperation since the end of the Second World War, and another reflection of the declining political and economic grip of the state. The modern state system was born in Europe, and it is Europe that is showing the way in the kinds of cooperative ventures that are leading to its transformation. To suggest that Europeans are losing control to an opaque and undemocratic European Union is wrong. Rather, they are pooling responsibilities where it makes most sense, are retaining the best features of the state model, and are using the regional approach to open new opportunities. Regional integration has clearly had a resonance with others, and might even be regarded as another example of European soft influence; not everyone else may be seeking to exactly replicate the European template, but it remains the leading point of reference.

7 Europe as a Global Player

The idea that the European Union might be a major global power has surprisingly few takers. It rarely crops up in any of the debates about the current or future shape of the international system, where the United States retains its dominance and fascination continues to grow with the rise of China, India, Brazil and other emerging powers. Europe, meanwhile, is accused of being too parochial and introspective, of being too protectionist, and of falling behind in its preparations for the world of tomorrow. Europe, it seems, has become the past while Asia and Latin America are the future. And even when the EU's role in the world is discussed, it is often disdained. 'Does the EU count in the world?' asked Commission president José Manuel Barroso in 2010. Yes, he answered. 'But does the EU count as much as it should?' he continued. Not yet, he answered, because the EU was not doing enough to define and defend the European interest.[1]

There are two main reasons for the mismatch between prospect and reality. First, we remain – even in the market- and trade-driven age of globalization – infatuated with military power. No matter the questionable value of violence as a tool of statecraft, we remain more impressed with sticks than with carrots. Second, European leaders have been unable to do enough to build the policies and the institutional structure needed to help the EU be seen and heard on the global stage. Polls reveal that ordinary Europeans favour common foreign and security policies by overwhelming majorities, but their leaders have been unable to deliver. The EU has most of the tools it needs to project itself, including population, wealth, technology and military capabilities, but it lacks the organizational ability and the collective will to use them.[2]

The effect of these two problems has been to leave the EU draped in something of a cloak of invisibility. It is rarely seen or acknowledged in public, and it is routinely judged to have played only a marginal role in most of the critical international problems of the last 20 years, be they the Balkans, the Middle East, international terrorism, climate change or illegal immigration. And yet beneath that invisibility cloak is a substantial and complex global actor:

- The EU is the wealthiest marketplace in the world, with more than half a billion consumers, most of whom sit firmly in the middle class with all that this signifies in financial terms. China and India together may have nearly five times as many people, but they are on average a great deal poorer.
- If we add up the military budgets, personnel and assets of the EU member states we find that they have the second largest military in the world, backed up by first-class training and advanced weapons technology. The EU is streets ahead of China and India in this regard.
- The EU accounts for nearly one-third of global economic output, with a combined gross domestic product bigger than that of the United States, and almost twice the size of those of China and India combined. Even the poorest EU member state (Bulgaria) has a per capita GDP one-third bigger than that of China's and nearly five times bigger than that of India's.[3]
- It is the biggest trading bloc in the world, accounting for about one-fifth of global trade in goods and commercial services.[4]
- In spite of its problems, the euro is the only currency that approaches the US dollar in terms of political and economic gravity. No one else – not even the Chinese – has anything to compare.
- The EU is the world's biggest source of, and target for, foreign direct investment, accounting for two-thirds of all investment flows involving OECD (Organization for Economic Cooperation and Development) member states.[5] This is a reflection both of the opportunities that foreign companies see in Europe, and of the confidence and reach of European companies.
- It is the world's biggest market for corporate mergers and acquisitions, its single market having encouraged the rise of new European multinationals that compete aggressively with their American and Japanese counterparts.
- It is the world's biggest source for official development assistance, accounting for more than half of all the funds made available by major donor countries.[6]

Considered individually, the bigger EU member states are still prominent members of the big international clubs, such as G7 and NATO, but they are not what they once were: Germany's economic clout has not translated into much political influence outside Europe, France's glory days are long gone, and any Briton who still believes in a 'special' political relationship with the United States is delusional. When taken as a group, however, and factoring in the international clout of the single market and EU trade policy, the member states exert an entirely different dynamic. In this era of globalization, the multinational, and problems such as climate change and poverty (for the solution of which large militaries are irrelevant), the collective qualities of the EU come into their own. Working together has the potential to allow the member states to exert enormous influence, and it is in their interests to see such influence better defined and expressed.

If the EU is still punching below its weight on the security front, on the economic front it is an entirely different matter. If its member states still occasionally go their own way on foreign policy, or if the EU routinely sits in the shadow of American power, everyone wants access to the single market and the EU is impossible to ignore on trade matters, where it acts as one and is seen as such by those with whom it trades. It set itself the goal of agreeing a common trade policy with the Treaty of Rome, and on the foundations of the single market has developed common positions that have allowed it to wield enormous global economic influence.

The single market in turn cleared the way for a programme of mergers and acquisitions that has created European corporations with global reach. Big is not necessarily best, and we are all familiar with stories of corporate greed and abuse of power, but this is one area where size matters a great deal. Europe before 1914 had markets whose links paved the way for the creation of large companies, but two world wars broke up those markets, and meant a loss of competitive advantage and European companies lost out first to the Americans and then to the Japanese. It was only with the incentives and opportunities created by the single market that European corporate leaders (and national governments) removed their national blinkers and rediscovered the need to merge with companies in other European states so as to regain their competitive and inventive edge. The results have been momentous.

Europe's International Presence

The biggest handicap that the EU faces in building a clear international presence is the persistence with which power in the world continues to be defined in military terms. We saw earlier how the EU is a civilian rather than a military actor, but much of the rest of the world has not yet caught up with this conceptual change. The EU is often overlooked simply because it lacks a combined military with which to back up its claims to be a major player, and because much of what it achieves instead comes out of international conferences that rarely capture news headlines. And it is not only overlooked, but is actively disparaged for the modesty of its military power and the assumption that it must continue to rely on, or defer to, US security guarantees. In his final policy speech before stepping down as US Secretary of Defense in 2011, Robert Gates warned of the lack of political will among its European members to commit sufficiently to NATO, the division between those who were prepared to fight and those who were not, and the dwindling patience of the United States, where policymakers might be tempted to conclude that the return on US investment in NATO was not worth the cost.[7]

The second handicap is the fuzzy shape of the EU on the radar of international relations. Many still think of it – in foreign policy terms, at least – as a cluster of individual member states rather than as a club, a problem exacerbated by its modest record in achieving institutional focus and by the frequent inability of its leaders to agree policy. Former US Secretary of State Henry Kissinger is purported once to have asked who he should call if he wanted to speak to Europe. He has denied saying it, but as the Italians would have it, *se non è vero, è ben trovato* (even if not true, it is a good story). Another American – George W. Bush – put it differently when, during a visit to the European Parliament in Strasbourg, he was reported to have commented that 'you guys sure have a lot of presidents'.

When a crisis breaks, we expect someone to be step up and explain the response and provide leadership, but the EU lacks such a person; the 1999 creation of a European high representative for foreign affairs failed to bring much change, and although the office was given new powers in 2009 and backed up with the formation of the European External Action Service (a European diplomatic corps), we still hear little from the high representative. At least part of the problem stems from the inadequacies in the sharing of intelligence, which has roots in the different ways in which it is gathered by member states of the EU and the absence of a standardized approach to information management.[8] The problem, once again, is not that integration has gone too far but that it has not gone far enough.

But this does not mean that there has not been progress:

- The EU's Common Foreign and Security Policy provides an account of the principles upon which the EU approaches international affairs: these include an emphasis on diplomacy to resolve international conflicts, a preference for peacekeeping over peacemaking, and recognition that because the EU has no standing army it must rely on its member states for the ad hoc contribution of military forces to help with disarmament, stabilization, crisis management, advising and humanitarian and rescue missions.
- The Common Security and Defence Policy has the goal of giving some substance to the EU's policies, specifically by developing the civilian and military means to take part in peacekeeping and crisis management.
- The European Security Strategy lists threats such as terrorism, weapons of mass destruction, failed states and organized crime, and calls on EU member states to be more strategic and coherent and to 'be ready to share in the responsibility for global security'.
- The European Neighbourhood Policy gives neighbouring states privileged access to EU investments and the single market in return for progress on democracy, human rights, the rule of law, good governance, free market reforms and sustainable development.

Each of these policies can be challenged for having provided the European global presence with too little substance, but at least they offer a framework upon which to build. And anyone who believes that even the biggest and most powerful of the EU's member states working alone can exert greater influence on international policy is in denial; none have either the military or the economic power to be more than middle-level players. And those who would argue that European interests are best served by working with (that is, following the lead of) the United States are overlooking hard realities. While Americans and Europeans work together more often than not, their perspectives are often too different: US administrations rarely show much more than a polite interest in what individual EU states have to say on international affairs, the US has been looking with more interest of late towards the Pacific, and the realist tradition in US foreign policy – which emphasizes rational self-interest and distrusts long-term cooperation and alliances – is out of step with the more multilateral perspective of the Europeans.

There being greater strength in numbers, EU states can achieve more working together as a group than individually, cooperation offering several clear advantages. Prime among these is the louder voice that can be enjoyed by a group of more than two dozen states containing more than half a billion people. Cooperation also offers the smaller member states of the EU the ability to have an impact on international affairs that would be largely denied to them if they worked alone; 12 of the EU member states each have a population of less than eight million people, and small economies to match, which they could rarely hope to leverage into global influence. As Winston Churchill once said, cooperation means that 'small nations will count as much as large ones and gain their honour by their contribution to the common cause'. There are also efficiencies to be gained from joint policy: bringing the resources and talent of multiple member states to bear allows the EU to explore a wider range of options and opportunities, to build on comparative advantage, to build networks, to take advantage of shared expertise and culture, and to minimize duplication.[9] Since 2004, for example, the European Defence Agency has helped improve the EU's military capacity by encouraging an integrated approach that identifies weaknesses, better channels research, and encourages the pooling and sharing of resources.

Working together on policy also encourages a consensus approach to policy, and while this can sometimes dilute its effects and slow down decision making, it has also created a distinctive European policy style that has risen above the narrow and insular to embrace the broad and universal. Europeans have become used to working together and achieving compromises, which has in turn helped encourage in them a habit of cooperation and a preference for diplomacy and negotiation over coercion and violence. This is good not just for Europeans but for international relations more generally. Unlike large states pursuing self-interest and perhaps being tempted

---

Box 12: Five benefits of a European foreign policy

1. Allows the EU member states to use their combined influence.
2. Allows smaller EU states to take part in large international debates.
3. Allows multiple member states to bring different skills and resources to policy, and encourages pooling and sharing while minimizing duplication.
4. Encourages diplomacy and cooperation rather than violence and coercion.
5. Promotes an inclusive consensus rather than the exclusive and self-interested preferences of individual member states.

---

to set aside the niceties of negotiation, the EU emphasizes rules-based solutions to international problems, and has been working to remake international relations in its own image.[10]

Unfortunately, the EU's foreign policy achievements are not always obvious, and the problem here is mainly one of understanding the unfamiliar; few know what to think of the EU because it is so unusual. But this can be an advantage. As one analyst puts it, 'the EU is not attempting to compete militarily with other world powers, the EU is not building up a military capacity independent of that of its member states, the EU is not trying to acquire [weapons of mass destruction], the EU has no territorial claims to make, the EU does not intend to intervene militarily to change regimes, and the EU is determined to work hand-in-hand with the United Nations'. In short, the EU is a new kind of global actor with approaches that are different from those we usually associate with great powers.[11] We are so used to the old way of doing business, however, that the EU leaves most of us puzzled, and we do not readily see or understand what it does.

Consider the example of official development assistance (ODA), of which the EU is the collectively the biggest supplier in the world: 54 per cent of the total provided by the world's major donor countries in 2011, or \$72 billion, came from EU member states, and a further \$13 billion was channelled through the EU institutions.[12] This is all the more impressive when we look at the amount of assistance in relation to the size of donor economies: of the five countries that have met the UN goal of aid totals equivalent to 0.7 per cent of GDP, four of them – Denmark, Luxembourg, the Netherlands and Sweden – are in the EU, and the rest of the member states are committed to achieving that goal by 2015 (an uphill struggle given current economic woes). The EU as a group also gives far more ODA than the United States (which has an economy almost as big), and while the US more than makes up for the difference with private flows of aid ($168 billion in 2011, compared to $94 billion from EU states[13]), much of that aid comes with ideological or religious strings attached, and as a result plays a more limited role in advancing US foreign policy interests.

The many questions about the efficacy of aid are well known,[14] and there is something repugnant about the EU (and the United States) limiting their aid budgets while subsidizing their own farmers and industries, thereby raising the bar for African farmers and entrepreneurs. But until such time as alternatives are pursued, there is more prospect of ODA being effective if multiple countries pool resources, collectively design policy, reduce duplication, and bring more ideas and a wider set of perspective to bear. EU aid still comes from the separate member states, but it is guided by a set of common policies and goals that give it more coherence. The eradication of poverty is at the top of the list, which also emphasizes values such as respect for human rights, fundamental freedoms, peace, democracy, good governance, gender equality, the rule of law, solidarity and justice, and a commitment to effective multilateralism. The EU once followed the lead of international organizations such as the OECD, but it has increasingly set the pace on aid policy, the joint approach allowing the Commission to be present in more places than the individual EU member states, and allowing the EU to exert more political cal influence.

The soft qualities of EU policy have been further reflected in its support and observation of elections in more than three dozen countries, including Afghanistan, Bolivia, Ecuador, Guinea-Bissau, Lebanon, Malawi, Mozambique, Pakistan, Russia and South Africa. As a group of states it has greater credibility than an individual state, which might be seen to have a political agenda, although the EU has not so far been in the position to follow up on any flaws that it finds.[15] The EU also operated more than two dozen police and military peacekeeping missions between 2003 and 2012, including those in Afghanistan, Bosnia, the Central African Republic, Chad, the Democratic Republic of Congo, Georgia, Guinea-Bissau, Indonesia, Kosovo, Macedonia, Moldova, Palestine and Ukraine, and an anti-piracy operation in the Indian Ocean. Again it has a communal credibility in this regard that would be denied most large individual states working alone.

The EU has also agreed common positions on a wide range of more focused international issues. For example, it championed the creation in 2002 of the International Criminal Court, and while not itself a party to the ICC statute (although all its member states have signed up) has since been the court's largest funder and most vocal supporter, prompting some to describe the ICC as an 'EU court'.[16] The EU has also been strongly supportive of efforts to develop an arms trade treaty under UN auspices that would establish international standards for the import, export and transfer of arms. Even Britain, with its large arms industry, is supportive of the treaty, offering a contrast to the United States, where the gun rights lobby has been able to whip up enough opposition in the US Congress to block ratification, even though the treaty would have no impact on domestic law.

It is also worth noting that in spite of the apparent modesty of the EU's work on the foreign policy front, Europeans are overwhelmingly in favour of a shared approach. This places them at odds with their leaders, as we saw with the embarrassment of the split over the 2003 US-led invasion of Iraq: while some governments supported the invasion and others were opposed, Europeans were by large majorities – and in every European country where polls were held – opposed to the invasion.[17] More recent polls have found that a common defence and security policy is supported by 75 per cent of Europeans and opposed by only 17 per cent, while a common foreign policy is supported by 64 per cent and opposed by only 25 per cent.[18] Meanwhile, two in every three Europeans believe that foreign and defence policies are better decided jointly at the EU level, compared to less than a third who still opt for policymaking at the national level. In only three countries (Finland, Sweden and the UK) is there still majority support for national policymaking, in contrast to the nearly 75 per cent in Germany and France who support an EU approach.[19]

How would European states have fared on the foreign and security policy stage had the EU never come into being? They might have found their policies converging as their economic ties grew in the wake of post-war reconstruction, and most would have felt the pressures for cooperation arising out of membership of NATO, but they would have found it more difficult to build the agreement needed to offer a shared face to the rest of the world. They would not have built the organizational connections or the habits of working with each other on policy. They would also have found it more difficult to be taken seriously by the United States and other world players, and to promote the kinds of rules-based and multilateral approaches that most Europeans instinctively favour over the more self-interested and military options that have long been at the heart of great power politics.

And what might a country that chose to leave the EU stand to lose by that decision? For Tony Blair, it is a matter of 'brutal realpolitik'. Against the background of a rising China and India, which by 2020 will have a combined population more than five times bigger that of the EU and nearly 35 times bigger that of Germany, the heft of the EU is needed in order to leverage power. Within the EU, he argues, a country like Britain counts for more, and without it, it counts for less. 'Politics at the top international level is about power,' he notes. 'Separate [Britain] out from the decision-making structure of Europe and we will immediately relegate ourselves in the league of nations.' And the idea that even one of the bigger European states could seek new bilateral relationships with the likes of China and India, he suggested, is an 'especial illusion', because neither will subordinate their relationship with Europe to one with an individual European country.[20]

Europe as a Trading Bloc

Even if there are clear limits to the EU's global military footprint, it is impossible to deny the size and reach of its global economic footprint. Taken individually, even the biggest EU member states are only second-ranking players in the global marketplace; Germany, France, Britain and Italy were, respectively, the 4th, 5th, 7th and 8th biggest economies in the world in 2011 (see Figure 7). But combine the member states and the result is an economic bloc with a GDP that is bigger than that of the United States, two and a half times bigger

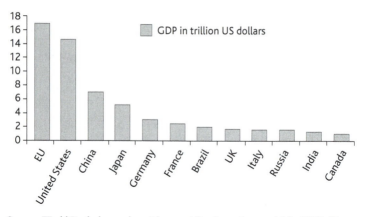

Source: World Bank data at http://data.worldbank.org (accessed July 2012). Figures are for 2011.

Figure 7   The world's biggest economies

than China, seven times bigger than Brazil, and nearly ten times bigger than India.

And this really is a case where size matters: big economies with large numbers of companies and consumers drive the global economic system and are key players in trade, investment and growth, as we see in the case of the United States. China and India may have vast populations and may be undergoing rapid economic growth (not so difficult when they are starting from a smaller base), but Europeans are far wealthier and more productive on a per capita basis, and have far more disposable income. Access to the European marketplace is irresistible and essential for any business seeking large pools of consumers and large potential profits. The Chinese and Indian markets may be growing faster, and will one day be world leaders, but that day is not yet here.

Trade has been one of the clear successes of the European project. At home, the opening of internal borders has boosted trade among the EU member states: as a share of all EU trade, intra-EU trade grew from 49 per cent in 1960 to nearly 64 per cent in 2010[21]), with all the resulting benefits to domestic consumers and business. Externally, the EU has a common trade policy that manages relations between the EU and third parties, and that has been highly effective. Trade has indeed been described as the very raison d'être of the EU and the quality that most obviously defines it as a civilian power.[22] It is one policy area in which the EU comes closest to having a single and clearly definable international personality, such that while European trade negotiations were once conducted mainly among EU member states, they are now conducted mainly between the EU and third parties.[23]

Another of the paradoxes in the debate about Europe is that while the EU's efforts on the foreign policy front have been studied closely and much written about (hence the joke that there may be more people studying that policy than actually working on it), its successes on the trade front have passed mainly unremarked. Although two-thirds of Europeans believe that the EU has benefited from international trade, only 44 per cent realize that it is the biggest player in world trade, while more than a third do not.[24] And not only is it the biggest player, but its achievements and influence have been considerable, showing how the collective whole can be greater than the sum of the parts.[25] By itself, for example, Germany is an impressive trading power, ranking second in the world for trade in commercial services and third for trade in merchandise, with France and Britain not far behind.[26] At a negotiating table where Germany, France and Britain are individually represented, in other words, all three will be taken seriously. But where there is a single trade negotiator representing the EU, which accounts for the biggest share of trade in the world (see Table 3), others will pay much closer attention.

Table 3   The world's three biggest trading powers

	% Share imports		*% Share exports*
Merchandise			
EU-27	16.2	EU-27	14.9
United States	12.3	China	13.3
China	9.5	United States	8.1
Commercial services			
EU-27	21.1	EU-27	24.7
United States	10.0	China	4.4
China	6.0	United States	13.9

Source: World Trade Organization, *International Trade Statistics 2011*, at www.wto.org (retrieved December 2012). Figures are for trade in 2011, and exclude intra-EU trade.

The advantages of a common EU policy are felt in two main areas. First, open economies grow faster than those to which access is restricted. Trade opens new opportunities, creates more jobs, gives consumers access to a wider set of goods and services at lower prices, increases competition, creates pressures for the removal of regulatory handicaps, and fosters efficiency and innovation. It also gives European companies more opportunities to invest abroad, and makes the European marketplace more attractive as a target for investment from overseas. But with the most vibrant markets now being outside the EU, and particularly in Asia and Latin America, there is also a clear need to work against protectionism and unfair trading practices; as a warning, we have only to look at the example of China with its currency manipulation, its subsidies to industry, its theft of intellectual property, and its restrictions on exports of key raw materials. In dealing with these problems, the EU as a unit is in a far stronger position than its member states would be working alone (although we should not forget that the EU can itself be protectionist and self-interested in pursuit of its trade interests).

The trading power of the EU is particularly visible in the meeting rooms of the World Trade Organization, which has a dispute settlement process through which trade disagreements are investigated and judgements issued that are binding on the parties involved. It should come as little surprise that the greatest number of cases have been brought to the WTO by the two giants in the room – the EU and the United States – and more often than not against each other. They have tussled over issues as varied as hormone-treated beef, agricultural imports from Latin America, tariffs on steel imports, genetically modified organisms and subsidies to aircraft manufacturers. The EU has not always won, but as a group it has a far louder voice than would even its biggest individual states working alone.

The EU has also been exerting pressure on its trade partners (notably China) to open up their markets for public procurement (government contracts), which account for more than 10 per cent of GDP in industrialized economies and a growing share in emerging economies. Access is limited because governments prefer to contract with domestic suppliers, but the EU has strengths in many of the sectors for which government work is contracted (including public transport) and has been pressuring others to rethink their policies.

Box 13: Six benefits of a European trade policy

1. Brings the collective influence of all EU states to bear in trade negotiations.
2. Allows EU states to speak with a louder voice, to exert soft global influence and to pursue European interests.
3. Better positions the EU to deal with growing competition from Brazil, China, and India.
4. Encourages and creates new opportunities and markets, giving consumers access to a wider set of goods and services at lower prices.
5. Increases the pressure for the removal of regulatory handicaps and for the standardization of rules and policies.
6. Gives European companies more opportunities to invest abroad, and makes the European marketplace a more attractive target for overseas investment.

The second key advantage of a common EU trade policy lies in the negotiating power that it offers: using access to the single market as a carrot, the EU can oblige its trade partners to change their habits to suit European values and policies.[27] This might be seen as an example of the EU being overbearing and insensitive, but it could also be seen as simple common sense: in a game where everyone is seeking to promote their own best interests, and where competition is growing, Europeans are better advised to work collectively than singly. Backed by its own experience of market integration, for example, and in the face of a lukewarm response from the United States and opposition from developing countries, the EU has championed the so-called Singapore issues, named for the WTO conference in 1996 at which they were promoted; these involve encouraging competition, investment, free trade and access to public procurement.

The EU has pursued change in part by requiring that foreign companies wishing to sell their goods in the EU conform to its standards and procedures in regard to everything from working standards to development policies. It has also been able to use the negotiating power of the opportunities it creates within its trading partners through investments and job creation. Some of this might be achieved by the bigger EU member states working alone, but the scale of the markets and influence involved would be entirely different. Consider the following examples of the reach of the EU:

- A 1994 regulation establishes a procedure by which economic operators and EU member states can call on the Commission to respond to trade barriers implemented by third countries. If these can be shown to have been harmful, the Commission can take action on behalf of the injured parties.
- In 2007 the EU instituted its REACH programme, designed to control the introduction of new chemicals into the European marketplace: each must be registered and tested for risks to human health and the environment, and alternative testing methods are encouraged. While the rules apply most immediately to EU manufacturers, any foreign manufacturer wanting access to the European market must also comply. The effect has been to change chemicals policy not just at home but also abroad.

And it should also not be forgotten that the EU has negotiated a series of preferential and free trade agreements with most parts of the world. These have been signed with close neighbours such as Switzerland and Norway, and also with South Africa and several northern African and Middle Eastern states, and with South Korea, Mexico and Chile. Negotiations are under way with Canada, and agreements with the United States and Japan are under consideration. Such agreements mean reduced tariffs on EU exports, more jobs for trade partners and for EU companies, more money in the pockets of consumers in the trade partners, and more pressure for political change in those partners whose democratic records still need work. And reaching multilateral agreements is more efficient than a single European country negotiating bilateral agreements with multiple partners.

Europe's Corporate Presence

One of the lesser-known effects of the single market has been to encourage European companies to merge across internal borders, thereby allowing them to make better use of the greater opportunities provided by the single market. It has also strengthened their ability to compete more effectively with their American and Japanese peers, preparing for new competition from Brazil, China and India, offering large new investments in economic development, creating substantial new economic opportunities, and expanding the global reach of Europe. After lagging for many years, and thanks to the logic of integration, the size of the EU mergers and acquisitions market has equalled and occasionally overtaken that of the United States.

Big is by no means best, and the less desirable qualities of large corporations are well documented[28]: large size can lead to an accumulation of power in the hands of giants, which can control large segments of their respective markets. Large companies can also become belligerent and aggressive, working to build monopolies, abusing their dominant positions, and being so driven by the profit motive that they spare few efforts in their rush to exploit workers, manipulate governments, trample smaller competitors, work around safety requirements, promote harmful products, overlook the environmental effects of their operations and minimize their tax bills.

But life in the cut-throat world of the multinational is often a question of survival of the biggest as well as the fittest. Large companies are more able than smaller companies to spread risks by raising capital across multiple markets and adapting to meet the demands of different groups of consumers. They can exploit the best that different labour markets have to offer, using the skills of a highly educated workforce in some countries and of a low-skill and lesser-educated workforce in others. With the large amounts of capital they generate, large corporations also have more to invest in research and development, pushing forward the boundaries of technological development, promoting innovation, and creating valuable and useful new products.

The size and reach of large companies also helps them promote growth in their respective fields, increasing profits and national income, creating new jobs, hiring and rewarding the best talent, and exploiting the ideas and inventiveness of the best and the brightest in multiple communities. They can offer a greater range of benefits and professional opportunities to their employees, they can bring new and high levels of investment into communities that might not otherwise have such opportunities, they make large investments in the

---

Box 14: Big corporations and European influence

- The single market has encouraged European corporations to acquire and merge with others in neighbouring EU states.
- The effect has been to create large European companies that can better compete with non-European rivals.
- Large companies are better placed to spread risk, exploit differences in labour markets, generate large amounts of investment capital, create new jobs and innovate.
- The rise of European corporations is another example of soft power at work.

---

development of local infrastructure, and their presence can mean large new tax revenues for the countries where new facilities are sited.

In a broader sense, large corporations are champions of soft political and economic influence, they promote a cosmopolitan culture, and the economic webs that they weave across multiple states help reduce the kinds of pressures and stresses that might otherwise lead to conflict and war. We could argue that small is better and regard large corporations with suspicion and disdain, but international market forces guarantee that large corporations will always be with us, and – on the principle that if you cannot beat them, join them – the European corporate sector needs to be well represented in this often brutal world. The alternative would be to have global markets dominated by large American, Japanese and increasingly Indian and Chinese corporations, with all the economic, political and even cultural influence that would accrue to their home states.

European companies had a long history of global operations built on the strategic advantages offered by imperialism, but they lost much market share after the Second World War. Their post-war American and Japanese competitors were often more dynamic, daring, aggressive, egalitarian, diverse and inventive,[29] while European companies had a tendency to be nationalistic, hierarchical, conservative, and driven less by quantity than by quality.[30] And while American corporations had the advantage of a large and open domestic market that acted as a launch pad for overseas operations,

European businesses found themselves hamstrung in their efforts to cross even their closest borders by numerous handicaps. These included different regulations and standards, taxes that discriminated against cross-frontier mergers, capital gains taxes on assets transferred as a result of mergers, double taxation on company profits, little in the way of European company law and commercial contract law, limits on the movement of goods and services, and governments often anxious to defend their so-called national champions against competition or takeovers from foreigners, even if they were right next door. The result was that even as late as the 1980s European companies were mainly looking to acquisition and merger opportunities either within their home countries or outside Europe.[31]

The rise of the single market changed the nature of the game by expanding the opportunities and financial incentives for European corporations to cooperate, merge, or at the very least explore neighbouring market opportunities. EU initiatives resulted in changes to company laws and regulations, while the growth of the single market increased the number of consumers that business could reach. The number of intra-Community mergers began to grow and finally overtook the number of national mergers for the first time in 1989–90.[32]

The results are reflected in the statistics. While it is increasingly difficult to tie multinationals to a particular home country, the *Fortune* Global 500 list of the world's biggest corporations in 2012 revealed that 27 per cent were from the EU and 26 per cent were from the United States (see Figure 8). The long list of American companies that have for so long been staples of the international corporate world – including Ford, Hewlett-Packard, IBM, Apple, Boeing and Microsoft – has been joined of late by a long list of European names, including Airbus, Total, AXA, ING, Allianz, BNP Paribas, E.ON, Carrefour and HSBC. But while much has been achieved, there is still much to be done for Europeans to build on these changes; as noted in Chapter 3, there is still a culture and a legal framework in the EU that militates against entrepreneurial initiative and creativity. The corporate reach of Europe could be much greater with more changes in EU law and policy, particularly those that ease up the labour market and reduce the administrative costs of start-ups and the financial costs of failures.

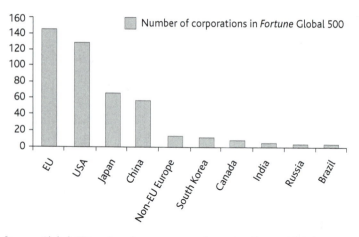

Source: Global 500 at http://money.cnn.com/magazines/fortune/global500/2011 (accessed December 2012).

Figure 8 The world's biggest corporations

As companies grow in size and reach, so there is more need to guard against abuses of dominant market position, particularly in fields overshadowed by a handful of large companies, such as pharmaceuticals, aerospace, motor vehicles and computers. And while such policies would normally be managed at the state level, once the construction of the single market was under way there had to be cross-border cooperation. This was a point not lost on the framers of the Treaty of Rome, who included competition policy on their shopping list. That policy has since been described as one of the flagship initiatives of the EU,[33] and it has helped make the European marketplace more open while also allowing the EU to flex its economic muscle overseas. The Commission can take action against efforts to restrict or distort the market (such as price fixing, illegal market-sharing or the abuse of dominant position), it can block or demand changes in plans for corporate mergers and acquisitions that might result in the creation of a new company with too big a share of the market, and it also keeps a close eye on government aid that might distort the market, such as subsidies, grants, contracts, tax and interest breaks, and government stakes in companies.

Recent examples of successful EU action include the fine levied on a group of pharmaceutical companies accused of trying to corner the global market in vitamins; charges against Nintendo for working to maintain high prices for its games consoles and cartridges; changing the terms of mergers between French petroleum giants TotalFina and Elf Aquitaine and pharmaceutical companies Pfizer and Pharmacia; the blocking of a proposed takeover by low-cost airline Ryanair of the Irish national airline Aer Lingus; and the pursuit of Microsoft for allegedly abusing its market dominance by squeezing out rivals to its Media Player and Internet Explorer. The EU has even been able to demand changes to plans involving companies in other countries; much to the chagrin of American policymakers, for example, it was able in 2000–1 to block a planned merger between US companies MCI/WorldCom and Sprint, and one between Honeywell and General Electric. The government of a single EU member state would have neither the political nor the economic clout to do this alone; it is the enormous size of the EU marketplace, and the fear of retaliatory action, that concentrates the mind of foreign governments and corporate behemoths.

With ongoing competition from the United States and Asia, and the rising competition posed by corporations based in emerging economies, European corporations need to exploit every opportunity they can to compete more effectively. They could have continued to do this through mergers and acquisitions within their home states and outside Europe, but it has also made sense for them to expand their base within the market that is closest to home. Had it not been for the single market, national corporations would have long continued to be handicapped. Even now, the entrepreneurial spirit of Europeans continues to be restricted by laws that promote a culture of risk aversion, and the difficulties of attracting venture capital. But while much remains to be done, the place of European corporations in the global marketplace has been much helped by the new opportunities created by regional integration.

8 Where to from Here?

Integrating Europe has never been easy. It was an ambitious and audacious project to begin with, it has had many problems along the way, and it will continue to face new problems (and fail to shake off old ones) indefinitely. It remains torn between efforts to unite and efforts to maintain national advantage, it is routinely misunderstood and misrepresented, there are competing ideas about what Europe is and what it should or might be, and it will always have its believers and its detractors. But to give them credit, the leaders of EU states and institutions have not been deaf to the doubts and criticisms, and have been creative in responding.

Forty years ago the EEC was being pilloried for spending too much on farm subsidies, to which governments replied with several hard-fought phases of reform that cut agricultural spending as a percentage of the EU budget. Thirty years ago it was being criticized for making too little progress on completing the single market; the response was an accelerated programme under the Single European Act to remove remaining barriers. Twenty years ago it was being mocked for its failure to achieve much on the foreign policy front; the response was several key policy initiatives and a reorganization of the way policy was made. It has most recently been shaken by the trials of the euro, the resolution of which has consumed more political energy than all Europe's earlier problems combined.

The list of difficulties remains long, and the solutions often seem frustratingly out of reach. But the greater the ambitions, the greater the challenges and also the greater the prospects of high rewards, assuming that all players keep their eyes on the ball. Many eyes have been taken off that ball of late, however, distracted by the cacophony of woe emanating from the euro zone, which has in turn fed off and been given new energy by a damaging combination of indifference and inattention. The euro zone crisis has undoubtedly been a game changer, and there can be no return to the old political and economic

146

order. But we must always remember Europe's accomplishments, the list of which – as this book has suggested – is long.

If the clouds surrounding the euro have a silver lining, it is that they have drawn new levels of public attention to the European project: more people have been following developments in Europe over a more sustained period of time than at any time in its history. What they have seen has not always been pretty, and has caused many to question their support for integration and their optimism for its future. And yet, by an overwhelming majority of 84 per cent to 11 per cent, Europeans believe that EU countries will have to work more closely together as a consequence of the crisis. By a factor of 63 per cent to 25 per cent, Europeans also believe that the EU has the power and the tools to defend the interests of Europe in the global economy. And more than half of Europeans believe that the EU will be stronger in the long run as a result of the crisis.[1]

The problems of the euro have spawned something of a cottage industry in scenario building, with numerous suggestions about where we might go from here. Many argue that Europe is now at the prosaic fork in the road, but the analogy is too simple and it would be more accurate to suggest that it has entered a roundabout from which – taking into consideration the wide range of political and public opinions about integration – there are at least five possible exits.

First, there is what we might call the doomsday exit, which would lead us to the end of the European Union. More than one political leader has suggested – perhaps in a fit of pique or in a moment of hyper-pessimism – that the collapse of the euro will mean the end of the EU. But while certainly not impossible, the end of the EU is highly improbable given the near-impossibility and undesirability of unravelling the many welcome and valuable ties that bind European states, backed up by the large numbers of Europeans who remain positive about the changes and hopeful about Europe's possibilities. The short-term economic and financial cost of closing down the EU would be enormous, bringing to mind a comparison with the nuclear option that for so long discouraged cold war leaders from committing to all-out war. Besides, why give up on the entire project in the face of the setbacks presented by the euro? Why undo the abundant benefits of regional integration achieved through so much hard work since 1952? The idea of returning to the era of border controls, restrictions on free movement, contradictory regulations, and European states tugging at the trouser legs of external powers is not one that most Europeans would entertain.

Even if the EU as a whole does not take this exit, the prospects of at least one of the bigger passengers (Britain) jumping out and taking this exit alone have recently become more real. Where once it was mainly Conservative party backbenchers and constituency groups who favoured this option, a poll in November 2012 found that 56 per cent of Britons would leave the EU if offered the opportunity in a referendum.[2] While it appeared that the long tradition of British euroscepticism was coming to a head, the news also sparked substantial commentary on how much Britain stood to lose from an exit, and also encouraged Europeans more generally to think more closely about the pros and cons of membership. It was clear from most of the commentary that individual member states could take little comfort from the option of a strategic withdrawal from the club, and that Britain in particular stood to lose far more than it might gain.

Second, there is the rollback exit. This might involve a rethinking of the terms of membership of the euro zone, the creation of a core of euro members with others sitting on the margins outside the euro zone, and a return to the basics of the single market. But this is all easier said than done, not least because the economic effects of leaving the euro are unclear, and economists have suggested that the cure would be far worse than the disease. Also, and as we saw earlier, it is near-impossible to identify the natural boundaries of the single market; the pressures of free trade will continue indefinitely to push integration into new areas of policy. And as we also saw, many of the problems of integration stem not from the process having gone too far so much as from the process not having gone far enough. Furthermore, there are broader pressures at work than the decisions of governments. Globalization, changes in information technology, initiatives by business, and the invisible hand of the global marketplace will keep nudging European states towards greater economic and political integration. And we should also remember that most of Europe's problems have been created not by the European institutions but by missteps on the part of national governments. The solution to these problems lies in advances, not retreats.

Third, there is the stagnation exit, which would take Europe back in the direction from which it has come. In other words, and assuming at least a minimalist binding of the wounds of the euro, Europe would continue muddling through, limping from one problem to another, making things up as it goes along, rounding corners without much more than an educated guess about what it will find, and all the time lacking much in the way of a plan. But this is the failed philosophy of the past, and even if there is agreement on little else, there is a consensus that the European project needs reform. Without a better sense of what Europe means and where it is headed, Europeans will fail to engage, the debate will continue to be dominated by a club of political and business elites, and eurosceptics will continue to misrepresent the meaning and effects of Europe, enjoying a level of influence out of proportion to their relative size. It is time that the EU was associated less with crises than with opportunities, and less with pessimism than with pragmatism. The past, then, needs to remain the past, and Europe needs new approaches and goals.

Fourth, there is the federal exit, which would take us down the road to a European superstate. Many think that Europe is already there, or very close, but it would take a great deal of change to create a truly federal Europe. Following a full fiscal and banking union for the euro zone, federalization would require full-scale reform of the EU institutions, giving them new powers and arranging for more direct elections to their senior offices. There would have to be an additional pooling or transfer of policy and lawmaking powers away from the parliaments of the member states, the Council of the EU might be reorganized as a new and elected Senate of the EU, there would be full-fledged EU foreign and economic policies, national embassies would be replaced by EU embassies, national passports would be replaced by EU passports, and national seats in all the key international organizations, such as the United Nations, would be replaced by EU seats.

But there is widespread resistance to the idea of a federal Europe, and taking this exit would do little more than intensify the backlash to integration that has been gaining ground since the early 1990s, as well as increasing the chances of departures from the EU by its more eurosceptic member states. And federalism by stealth, which eurosceptics charge has been going on for many years, is neither the democratic nor the honest alternative. Achieving an effective and popular federal Europe would demand the drawing up and agreeing

---

Box 15: Five exits from the European roundabout

1. Doomsday: dissolution of the European Union.
2. Rollback: a return to the basics of the single market.
3. Stagnation: keeping on muddling through.
4. Federal: the creation of a European superstate.
5. Confederal: confirmation of a European union of states.

---

of a federal constitution, a goal unlikely to be achieved against a background of the economic problems and distorted debate about Europe that prevail today. It will be many years, perhaps even decades, before the political climate will be right to even begin to have a sensible debate about a federal Europe. Rushing in too soon would result at best in a two-speed Europe, where some countries (mainly those in the euro zone) move ahead while others opt out altogether.

The fifth and final option option – which currently lacks a clear signpost and is not marked on most political maps – is the confederal exit. Again assuming at least a minimalist resolution of the euro zone crisis, this exit would mean formal agreement that the EU is a confederation, or a union of states where voters have indirect representation (the European Parliament excepted), member states retain a large measure of control over internal affairs (the single currency excepted), and governments continue working together on areas of policy where joint approaches make the most sense. True, it already has several federal elements, but just as federations come in many different forms with greater or lesser levels of centralization, so have history's confederations. That the EU is a confederation with federal elements need not discourage us from taking this exit.

The confederal option has the advantage of locking in the best of what the EU has achieved, providing a label by which Europeans might better understand and measure the work of the EU, assuaging the fears of those who oppose further integration, and minimizing opportunities for the work of the EU to be misrepresented. It would by no means solve all Europe's problems, but it would provide us with a benchmark against which the activities and goals of European integration could be measured with more accuracy. To this point,

Europe has been a ship following a course to an unknown destination. Opting formally for confederation would give us a nearby port that we could enter to effect repairs, tie up loose ends and reconsider plans, all the while undistracted by squalls and storms.

Something of a blueprint for how we might proceed has already been published in the form of the Laeken Declaration, agreed and issued by the heads of government of the member states in December 2001. True, Laeken did not have a happy outcome (it led to the failed constitutional treaty), and it offered more questions than answers, but that does not mean that its ideas are not worth revisiting. Combining the general goals of Laeken with the more detailed qualities of confederal administration, I make three sets of suggestions for where we go from here: Europeans need to be encouraged to engage more fully in the debate over Europe, European institutions need to be reformed so as to make them more efficient and responsive, and attention needs to be paid to completing the many items of unfinished business on the European agenda.

Public Opinion: Engaging Europeans

Europe will not succeed without the engagement of Europeans. For too long now, the European project has been designed and conducted by political and policy elites, leaving us with knowledge and engagement deficits that need to be narrowed, even if they cannot realistically be closed. Europeans need to feel more sense of investment in Europe, they need to be armed with a helpful balance of information regarding its advantages and disadvantages, and they need a better sense of what Europe represents. We can achieve much of this by deepening rather than widening, allowing the European project to settle, and allowing time for its flaws to be worked out in a considered fashion unpolluted by scepticism, pessimism, myths, misunderstandings and crises.

As a system of governance, the EU is far from unique in suffering a lack of public understanding. That many Europeans know little about their own national systems of government is reflected in the worried speculation about how many would fail the citizenship tests recently introduced in several EU countries for new immigrants. And the need for a better-informed citizenry has not escaped the attention of the European institutions; in a 2005 action plan, the Commission noted that there had been too much emphasis on messages that reflected political priorities rather than the interests of Europeans, and too many campaigns that focused on political elites and the media while failing to portray the benefits and consequences of the EU to ordinary Europeans in a direct and understandable manner.

The European institutions could certainly do a better job with communication, but while you can lead a horse to water, you cannot make it drink – not, that is, unless it is thirsty. Since thirst is generated by need, Europeans must first feel the need to understand the EU, which requires in turn that they must be confident that the European project matters, that it is not something constructed and maintained by elites, and that it has improved their lives rather than being a source of crises, red tape and threats to democracy. Perversely, controversy and bad news is more likely to engage public attention than efficiency and good news, and in this sense the euro zone crisis and talk of a potential British exit have provided a useful short-term service. But there is only so far that we can expect controversies to take us without creating a public that is hardened against European integration, and impatient with the spin placed on those controversies by supporters and opponents of Europe.

It has been suggested more than once that we might begin with the basics and do more to inject the EU into the school curriculum, thereby building new generations of Europeans that are more aware of the EU and have a better grasp of its possibilities and limitations. But this has been tried now for years with only limited success, and it anyway smacks of propaganda. And what is the purpose of teaching pupils about the EU if they cannot see for themselves how the EU matters and what impact it has had on their lives? Education should not be overlooked, but there needs to be a broader change in the way the EU is discussed and portrayed if Europe is to take its deserved place in the public consciousness.

In terms of helping improve understanding of the EU, what can we expect from the elites who are so often accused of running the project? It has been a long time since the debate over Europe produced leaders of the calibre of De Gasperi, Adenauer, Churchill, Schuman and Monnet. But they were working in a very different world in which news was channelled through a handful of sources. Today we have many more sources of information and many more people trying to make themselves heard, with fewer opportunities for strong leaders to show the way. The international political environment has also changed, such that European leaders can no longer speak only to domestic audiences but must think globally and respond to the new challenges of the global economy, the internet, and competition from emerging powers. Finally, the EU is designed to be government by committee, and while German leaders might occasionally rise above the pack by virtue of the size of the German economy, most other leaders are constrained by the nature of EU decision making as well as the difficulty of reaching out to people speaking several dozen languages.

Journalists constitute another elite, and have a critical role as opinion formers, but their fascination with bad news over good news has helped sustain the aura of pessimism that surrounds Europe. 'If it bleeds it leads,' runs the journalistic dictum, and the drama of a failed EU summit or a negative vote in a European referendum will capture the headlines more readily than data showing that European regional policy has improved prospects for unemployed Europeans (to the extent that such a claim could even be proved). More problematic, though, is the limited understanding of the experts: journalists exacerbate the confusion over Europe by the manner in which they are obliged to simplify often complex problems. Add to this the compartmentalization of news sources discussed in Chapter 4, with the overwhelmed consumer of news often seeking out only those sources that fit with their view of the world, and we soon see the limited possibilities of improved contributions to the debate from the media.

Academics make up yet another elite, and have an important role to play, but they too often speak only to each other. Academic accomplishment is measured more by the raising of research funds and publication in scholarly journals than by success in making new information or insights more widely available. Much academic research pushes forward the boundaries of knowledge and could help make us all wiser and less confused, but much of it goes unseen and unread by all but small communities of specialists, and much more is ignored because of the whims of academic fashion: if enough scholars latch on to an idea, all others working in the same area will feel obliged to refer to that idea, while other potentially useful ideas are left on the cutting-room floor. More perhaps than most, academics are the victims of communal reinforcement, confirmation bias, and an inclination to find comfortable seats on available bandwagons.

Having said, then, that there is a problem with engagement that stems from problems with education, communication, leadership, the media and academia, what is the answer? In short, it is change in all of the above. European institutions need to do a better job of explaining what they do and sparking engaged debate. Leaders need to remember what life is like outside the hothouse of decision making, negotiating and briefing. Journalists need to take more care over the way they portray the EU and over the variety of stories they cover, paying due attention to successes as well as failures. And academics need to step out of the ivory tower, occasionally set aside the pressures that define the reward systems within the academy, and make their work more widely comprehensible and available. With the elites being less elitist, we all have a better chance of understanding the issues at stake.

Institutions: Doing Better with What We Have

Just as great white sharks must keep moving in order to breathe and live, so all organizations – whether large or small – must constantly change and adapt in order to grow. There is rarely a time when they do not face troubles, or when opportunities for improvements cannot be found. To say that the EU needs reform, then, is like saying that humans need oxygen. The great past drawback that the European institutions have faced is that they have been built without a long-term plan. But they are more sinned against than sinning. That they are regarded with so many doubts (where they are regarded at all) is because they are poorly understood, are a convenient scapegoat for national politicians looking for something to blame for their own failures and inadequacies, and are an easy target for eurosceptics looking to demean the European project.

Numerous suggestions have been made for ways in which they might be reformed, ranging from changes in the number of European commissioners to the way commissioners are appointed, the way the EU budget is constructed and managed, the weighting of votes in the Council of the EU, the electoral system of the European Parliament, and even the salaries and expenses paid to MEPs. The Laeken Declaration offers a useful starting point:

Within the Union, the European institutions must be brought closer to its citizens. Citizens undoubtedly support the Union's broad aims, but they do not always see a connection between those goals and the Union's everyday action. They want the European institutions to be less unwieldy and rigid and, above all, more efficient and open. Many also feel that the Union should involve itself more with their particular concerns, instead of intervening, in every detail, in matters by their nature better left to Member States' and regions' elected representatives. This is even perceived by some as a threat to their identity. More importantly, however, they feel that deals are all too often cut out of their sight and they want better democratic scrutiny.

The suggestion most often made for improving the connections between Europeans and the European institutions is to more clearly define the leadership of the EU. This might be achieved through some kind of institutional rationalization, or by reducing the number of leaders, or by making those leaders more directly accountable to voters through elections. But while these suggestions would seem at first glance to have an attractive logic, recent experience suggests that we need to be careful how we proceed.

Beginning with the matter of rationalization, there was a time when responsibility for external relations was divided among four European commissioners who were given charge over separate geographical areas. While this might have seemed inefficient, it gave four member states the chance to have 'their' commissioner participate in decisions on external relations, and made sure that no single commissioner had the kinds of powers that would come with combining them into a single post. When, indeed, such a post was finally created in 1999, it had few substantial powers or responsibilities, and even since its reorganization in 2009, Europe's high representative for foreign affairs and security policy has failed to make much of a mark because of the desire of member states to keep their seats around the table at international meetings.

Consider also the example of the creation in 2009 of the new office of President of the European Council, designed to replace – with a single and clearly identifiable president – the cumbersome rotating presidency held for spells of six months by the leaders of each member state. The new post was handicapped from the beginning by its vague terms of reference: under the Treaty of Lisbon, the president is expected to 'drive forward' and 'ensure the preparation and continuity' of the work of the Council, to 'endeavour to facilitate cohesion and consensus' in the Council, and to represent the EU on foreign and security matters without stepping on the toes of the high representative for foreign affairs. Instead of appointing someone to the post with charisma, ambition and a high international profile (like Tony Blair, who was long considered a front runner but was tainted by being British and by having supported the Iraq war), the Council appointed incumbent Belgian prime minister Herman van Rompuy, who was neither charismatic nor ambitious but was skilled as a coordinator and consensus builder. He was, in essence, all that the egos of Council members would allow, and in many ways was perfect for the job.

We could reduce the number of presidents, and administrative confusion, by combining the jobs of president of the European Commission and European Council, but this would remove the separation of responsibilities that currently exists between the Commission and the Council, thereby combining more authority in the hands of one person than – again – most national leaders (and eurosceptics) could accept. We could also consider keeping the two positions separate, but making one or both subject to direct elections by European voters. But either option would create new administrative tensions between the Commission and the Council, would make the EU even more like a federal United States of Europe than it already is, and would present candidates with the problem of explaining to European voters how the responsibilities of the two offices differed.

As for any suggestion that the legitimacy and democratic responsiveness of the EU might be improved by direct elections to some of the top posts in the EU hierarchy, the example of elections to the European Parliament does not augur well. Even as the powers of the EP over the lawmaking process have grown, turnout at elections has fallen, a problem that has (ironically) been used to cast doubts on the legitimacy of Parliament. Voters do not turn out at EP elections in part because so many do not understand what Parliament does, but also – more importantly – because there is no change of government at stake as there is in national elections. The only way to change this would be to tie the party make-up in the EP to the membership of the European Commission, but this would have the effect of giving the president of the Commission an electoral mandate and thus giving the position new powers and credibility that – yet again – most national leaders (and eurosceptics) would find hard to stomach.

In short, then, there is too much political resistance to either reducing the number of presidents or having some or any of them directly elected by voters. But then what is so wrong with the status quo?

- We have a president of the Commission, whose job is to run the bureaucracy of the EU, oversee the process by which new laws and policies are proposed and implemented, and convert the generalities of the treaties into specific actions.
- We have a president of the European Council, whose job is to move the members of the Council toward agreement.
- We have presidents of the European Parliament and the European Court of Justice, whose job is to make sure that their two institutions carry out their respective charges.
- We have the presidency of the Council of the EU resting in the hands of a six-month rotation among the member states. This can be messy and lumpy, but it helps ensure that the member states remain engaged in the European project.
- We have a separation of powers that offers a balance between the interests of the member states, of Europe more generally, and of the voters of the EU.
- We have a system which ensures that not too much power or authority is placed in the hands of a single office or officeholder.

Institutionally, then, there is nothing mortally wrong with the way the EU is structured. There is, instead, something wrong with the tripartite relationship between the European institutions, the governments of the member states, and Europe's citizens. The Laeken Declaration said it well when it noted that the EU needed to become more democratic, more transparent and more efficient, and that the priority was to 'clarify, simplify and adjust the division of competence' between the EU and the member states, and that this might lead to a restoration of some responsibilities to the member states while giving new missions and powers to the EU.

Laeken also talked of the need to simplify the existing European treaties without changing their content, and the unfortunate end result was a constitutional treaty that was widely seen as going beyond this charge. When it was rejected by French and Dutch voters in 2005, the governments of the member states responded by sneaking most of the changes through as the supposedly revamped Treaty of Lisbon. With all the adjustments they considered necessary thus adopted, and many Europeans still boiling with resentment at the less than honest means used, now is not the time for any new treaties, which would involve too many new departures. Now is instead the time to allow the core institutional structure of the EU to develop some roots and routines, and to encourage Europeans to exploit the numerous channels they have available to engage with Europe, without the kinds of distractions created by crisis and controversy.

Policies: Taking Care of Unfinished Business

In addition to the problems of perception and engagement, Laeken also made the point that the EU was having trouble adjusting to the realities of a rapidly changing and globalized world. Does Europe, asked its authors, not have 'a leading role to play in a new world order, that of a power able both to play a stabilizing role worldwide and to point the way ahead for many countries and peoples?' The EU should be working against violence, terror and fanaticism, they went on, while also addressing injustice and 'seeking to set globalization within a moral framework'.

The Declaration noted that the image of a globally engaged Europe had wide public support, and that there had been calls for a greater EU role in everything from combating poverty and social exclusion to creating jobs, protecting the environment, taking action against cross-border crime, controlling migration flows, and helping asylum seekers and refugees (all 'transnational issues which [Europeans] instinctively sense can only be tackled by working together'), as well as support for a greater European involvement in foreign affairs, security and defence. In short, the Declaration concluded:

> ... what citizens understand by 'good governance' is opening up fresh opportunities, not imposing further red tape. What they expect is more results, better responses to practical issues and not a European superstate

or European institutions inveigling their way into every nook and cranny of life. In short, citizens are calling for a clear, open, effective, democratically controlled Community approach, developing a Europe which points the way ahead for the world. An approach that provides concrete results in terms of more jobs, better quality of life, less crime, decent education and better health care. There can be no doubt that this will require Europe to undergo renewal and reform.

The message is clear: the key to the success of Europe is not more and worse but less and better. We need a Europe that is leaner and fitter, which means placing it on a policy diet requiring that it focus only on what it does best. The governments of the member states and the European institutions – held more accountable by a newly engaged European citizenry – need to work on making the European project more efficient. This would allow more time for sober reflection and discussion on the changes that Europe has brought, and improve the prospects of debate based more on hard realities than on the interpretation of elites and sceptics with narrow agendas.

Europe can sometimes seem like one of those old homes that someone buys and renovates, but instead of seeing every project through to completion, the owners get distracted or impatient and move from one job to another, completing some but leaving many

---

Box 16: A shopping list for policy reform

- Addressing the flaws in the structure and management of the euro.
- Removing the remaining barriers to the single market.
- Closing the gaps in the European transport system.
- Allowing changes to the EU foreign policy-making structure to take root and evolve.
- Building on the soft power advantages of Europe.
- Reaching more common positions on foreign policy and making it better known what Europe represents and stands for.
- Continuing with reforms to agricultural and fisheries policy.
- Building on the achievements of environmental policy, and providing more leadership on climate change.

unfinished. The focus of policy in the EU should be on returning to those unfinished jobs and taking care of them. Only then will the residents of the house be able to see the bigger picture. And only when they have a better sense of its structure and how it all fits together, and have had a break from the discomfort of living in a permanent building site, should they start thinking about major new projects.

The biggest and most important unfinished project is the single market. There are still too many barriers to the free movement of people, money, goods and services, which undermine the ambitious Europe 2020 plan to make the EU a smarter, more inclusive and more sustainable economy by reducing unemployment, improving investments in research and development, reducing greenhouse emissions, increasing energy efficiency, improving education records, and reducing poverty and social exclusion. The single market is the one major project on which most Europeans can agree, and a return to the basics of deeper market integration holds out the promise of providing them with a goal that can unite rather than divide, as well as helping the EU recover from the effects of the global financial crisis and the euro zone crisis.

We saw earlier in the book that while there have been achievements on many different fronts, economic development and job creation continues to be handicapped by limits on market integration. Prime among these have been the ongoing barriers to the free movement of workers, combined with worries about high unemployment – particularly among younger workers – and tepid levels of productivity. There are also worries about the effects of a combination of growing life expectancy and declining birth rates, which is altering the balance between workers and retirees. There needs to be more flexibility and security (flexicurity) in labour markets, retraining in order to provide people with new skills for the changing economy, improvements in working conditions, and more investments in the kind of pan-European educational policies that the EU has been pursuing.

There also needs to be a new effort by European governments to open up the market in services, more changes designed at encouraging business start-ups, and more rapid progress in opening and expanding the opportunities for e-commerce. There are also still too many holes in the European transport network, where more needs to be done to exploit the impressive changes of the last few decades. Building new highways and high-speed railway lines will connect more parts of the EU to each other, making it easier to get goods to market and encouraging investment in the poorer states, and the poorer parts of richer states.

The success of the single market has long been predicated on the availability of a single currency, and while it goes without saying that the management of the euro needs much work, it is also worth repeating that the euro is in essence an excellent idea that has suffered the twin blows of design flaws and unhappy circumstances. The design flaws would have come to light eventually; the global financial crisis of 2007–10 made sure not only that they were revealed sooner but also that policymakers were woefully unprepared to respond. There has been a steep learning curve since the breaking of the Greek debt problems in 2009, and while we are not yet out of the wood, we know far more about the dynamics of monetary integration today than we did then. Whether the euro continues to weather the storm until it reaches calmer waters, or whether we see some tactical exits or excisions, there is much that can and should be saved, and with the benefits of new insight and stricter requirements on budgetary discipline, no reason why a leaner and stronger euro should not emerge.

The second most important unfinished project is foreign policy. Efforts to move Europeans onto the same page date back to the 1960s, and while there has been a plethora of grand-sounding initiatives, including the common foreign, security and defence policies, the EU continues to punch below its weight. In terms of the balance of international power, this is a time of great change: the United States is neither as powerful nor as credible as it once was thanks to its political and economic woes and its troubled ventures in the Middle East; China is clearly undergoing a massive growth spurt but it remains unclear where this will take it; Russia sits glowering and enigmatic on the edge of the stage; and India has the potential for great power if only it could impose some order on its economic house.

However events unfold, Europeans need to be heard. There have been many positive changes in the structure of EU policymaking, including the redefinition of the work of the high representative for external relations, and the construction of the EU diplomatic corps, the European External Action Service. Both need to be allowed to develop without the distractions of damaging internal political squabbles, and the EU needs a long spell free of the effects that such crises have had on undermining its credibility. The EU is the wealthiest marketplace in the world and the pre-eminent practitioner of civilian approaches to international relations. It is also the only global actor in a position to offer credible liberal alternatives to the often realist qualities of US foreign policy, and the only one capable of giving US foreign policymakers the occasional reality check.

Grand visions and general policies are not the way to go. The EU needs to continue exploiting its soft power advantages, which means continuing to be an economic magnet, exploiting its advantages in international trade, generating and attracting foreign direct investment, continuing to take on the corporate behemoths of the United States, Japan and China, and generally making the most of its brand as a source of opportunities and incentives rather than threats and violence. It also needs to continue building on its common foreign policy positions and carving out a niche for itself as a military power that ranks peacekeeping above peacemaking.

There are plenty of additional policy areas that could stand either doses of reform or greater injections of political focus and determination. On agricultural policy, for example, the EU has come a long way since the bad old days of butter mountains, wine lakes and wasteful subsidies, but the need for further reform is clear. On fisheries policy, the EU has managed to fall short of its core goal of sustainability while also annoying almost everyone involved in the fishing industry. On environmental policy, there has been rapid progress since national governments finally discovered the environment in the 1970s, but there is still much to do, not least in confirming the EU as the global leader on climate change.

Overall, the problems of the euro should not blind us to the many areas of policy where there has been a long history of European cooperation, and where such cooperation makes sense and has little political or public opposition, even if there is always room for improvement. The residents of that imaginary house need to cut back on all the grand plans and new projects, acknowledge the size and shape of the house for what it is, and deal with all those unfinished projects in a methodical fashion. The results would be far better for everyone who called it home.

9 Twenty Reasons Why Europe Matters

There is a scene in Monty Python's *Life of Brian* in which two activists complain about the Roman imperialist state and ask their audience what the Romans have ever done for them, other than bleed them white and take everything they ever had. The audience starts to offer suggestions. Romans provided the aqueduct, says one. Sanitation, says another. The list continues: roads, irrigation, medicine, education, health, wine, public safety and peace. All right, responds the leading character in frustration, but apart from all that what have the Romans really done for them?

It can sometimes seem that Europe faces the same problem of unrecognized contributions. What has it done for us, ask its critics, apart from chipping away at national sovereignty, undermining national identities, promoting government by unelected bureaucrats, and tying Europe in bundles of red tape? In this book I have argued that Europe has in fact given us (Europeans and non-Europeans alike) a great deal, but that we have not always been good at appreciating this. Distracted by the misunderstanding and misrepresentation that colours much of the debate about Europe, it has been easy to conclude that Europe is elitist, undemocratic, opaque, unpopular and inefficient. But this is not so. The European project has had its share of problems, to be sure, but this is less because it is inherently misguided or imprudent than because it has been made up on the fly, has no agreed end-state, and defies easy definition. In the resulting welter of uncertainty, euroscepticism has thrived and Europe has been battered by the slings and arrows of indifference and misinformation.

In the preceding chapters I have listed and supported the many reasons we have to celebrate Europe, and the ways in which we can make it better. Most of the achievements can be credited to the work of the European Union, under whose auspices we have seen life for Europeans improved both quantitatively and qualitatively. Some of these changes have had focused effects, others have meant more general benefits for the member states of the EU, yet others have had a global reach, and some have been easier to measure than others. In the pages that follow, I summarize – in the order in which they appear in the book – the 20 most important reasons why Europe matters.

1: Replacing Self-interest with Shared Interests

History has bequeathed to us a habit of ordering societies into states. They work well much of the time, and help us impose order on what might otherwise be a disorderly world of competing and often ambitious human wants and needs. But they also impose artificial divisions on society, encourage us to pursue narrow interests at the expense of the general welfare, impede the free movement of people, money and ideas, are often unable to guarantee the security of their citizens except through intimidation and threats against other states, have an unfortunate history of going to war with one another, have only a mixed record in dealing with problems common to different states, and often oblige people from different backgrounds and with different values to live together.

The EU has helped us rise above all this. It offers us a confederal arrangement that retains and protects many of the organizational advantages of states while helping us avoid many of their drawbacks. It has encouraged people to work together on shared or common problems while at the same time allowing for the coexistence of communities, regions, nations, states, and Europe itself. This network of identities allows Europeans to celebrate and maintain their differences while reminding them how much they have in common, how much they are invested in each other's welfare, and how working together is almost always preferable to working in isolation.

Little of this would have happened without the EU. Cooperation has been a hallmark of relations among democracies in other parts of the world, but they continue to place self-interest first, just as Europeans did for centuries. Without integration, Europeans would have continued to identify mainly with states and nations, and many would have continued to support the kind of nationalism that long brought so much strife and conflict to Europe, and that even today can make us overlook the broader global community of which we are all a part. The EU has encouraged in Europeans a worldview that is holistic and cosmopolitan to a degree found nowhere else in the world.

2: Adapting to Changes in the International System

The post-war era has been one dominated by the pressures of international cooperation, economic interdependence and globalization. Europe's larger individual states – and even some of its smaller ones – might have fared well in the face of these pressures without the European Union, but the ties of cooperation that have come in the wake of regional integration have placed them in a better position to assess, address and adapt to the changes. More than is true of many other parts of the world, Europe has had so much first-hand experience of cross-border cooperation that it has developed more effective instincts about the changing dynamics of the international political and economic environment. And the habits it has formed through cooperation have placed it in a stronger position to exploit and influence the opportunities that arise, and to address new challenges.

3: Bringing a Lasting Peace to Europe

Peace was always the cardinal goal behind the European project, the logic being that integration would build ties that – in the words of the Schuman Declaration of May 1951 – would make war 'not merely unthinkable, but materially impossible'. The causes of war and peace have never been firmly agreed, as we have seen, and the EU by itself cannot take all the credit for the peace that has prevailed in Europe since 1945. But it certainly deserves the lion's share, which is why it was awarded the Nobel peace prize for 2012 as recognition for its work over six decades in the advancement of peace, reconciliation, democracy and human rights in Europe.

Integration has encouraged peace in Europe by helping neutralize many of the causes of war, such as mistrust, opposing interests, and competition for power and resources. It has created a network of institutions, policies and laws that have encouraged voluntary habits of collaboration and cooperation. It has weakened the psychological and political links between Europeans and the states and nations of which they are a part, and which have long been one of the most persistent causes of war in the region. By opening up trade and encouraging cross-border investment, the EU has helped Europeans develop a vested interest in each other's welfare, making them more inclined to work together to solve problems and resolve disputes, and placing a premium on social investments over military investments. Most importantly, military power is no longer central to European identity, and Europeans do not just avoid going to war with one another but have no interest in going to war with others.

Peace might well have reigned in Europe without the European Union, if only because Europeans had tired of war by 1945, and the United States had a strategic interest in a peaceful Europe. But it would not have been the positive or perpetual peace we have today, because it would have been based more firmly on the maintenance of armies and military alliances. There would thus have been less prospect for the improvement of Franco-German relations that we have seen since 1945, and a cluster of divided western European states would have fared worse in recovering from the war or addressing the threats posed by the Soviet Union. And without the EU, Europeans would not have become global leaders in economic cooperation, or so quickly have removed barriers to free movement, or so effectively have learned to build a lasting trust in each other.

4: Offering a Benchmark Model of Civilian Power

Power and influence have long been defined by the capacity to inflict violence and to guard against the infliction of violence by one's enemies. Even today, it is the countries with the biggest or fastest growing militaries, such as the United States, China and India, that continue to most impress us with their raw power. But we have seen that military force has many disadvantages: it does not always prevail, it can be expensive in human and financial terms, it diverts resources away from more useful endeavours, it can create tensions where none might otherwise have existed, and there is little evidence that it brings durable and positive democratic change, and – given the changing nature of security threats – it is increasingly irrelevant. Willing and constructive behaviour, in other words, is unlikely to be encouraged at the end of a barrel of a gun.

Building on the distaste that many Europeans have felt since 1945 towards conflict and war, the EU has emerged as a benchmark for the promotion of influence through civilian rather than military means. Most European states maintain militaries, but they prefer to use diplomacy, encouragement and economic incentives to achieve their goals, turning to the military only as a last resort. They also prefer the use of soft power to shape rather than force change on others, using incentives and opportunity rather than threats and aggression. Against the contrasting example of the United States with its enormous defence budgets and powerful military-industrial complex, Europe's emphasis on peace, welfare, material well-being and social stability is clear and distinctive.

Civilian power has numerous advantages: it creates fewer threats and tensions than military power, it is more likely to bring durable democratic change, it is less costly in human and financial terms, it is more focused on constructive economic means to bring change, it is based on co-option rather than coercion, and it has more value and efficiency in dealing with problems such as poverty, disease and climate change. After centuries in which power and influence has been defined mainly by the size and use of militaries, Europe is today leading the way in replacing the philosophy of the warfare state with that of the welfare state.

5: Bringing Prosperity, Innovation, Opportunity and Choice

Even Europe's critics would in the main agree that the signal achievement of integration, and the clearest indication of why Europe matters, has been its single market. It is not yet complete or fully open, but enormous progress has been made in removing restrictive and protectionist barriers to the free movement of people, capital, goods and services. The benefits have been manifold: time-consuming border crossings are mainly gone, new jobs have been created, business has access to a bigger marketplace, consumers have access to a wider range of products and services at more competitive prices, competition has encouraged innovation, technical standards and regulations have been improved and reduced, and costly and protectionist national laws have been replaced with harmonized EU-wide approaches and standards. The problem today is not that the single market has gone too far but that it has not gone far enough: enormous possibilities await to be exploited – for example, in regard to the provision of services and the expansion of the digital marketplace.

The economic story of Europe would have been quite different without the EU. There would doubtless have been market pressures to reduce barriers to freer trade, just as there have been in other parts of the world, but many of the restrictions would still exist (as they do among the EU's major external trading partners), the European marketplace would be more fragmented, the opportunities provided to poorer EU members would have been more restricted, the differences in regulations and standards that most often interfere with trade would have been addressed only in a limited fashion, and efforts to encourage exchange rate stability (and so to clear the way to increased trade) would have proceeded in a more piecemeal fashion. Certainly the euro would never have been seriously considered, let alone actually have come into existence. Instead, and thanks mainly to the single market, the EU is today the world's wealthiest and most prosperous marketplace, and an irresistible economic magnet of a size and reach that allows the EU to exert soft influence on a global scale.

6: Promoting a Cleaner and Greener Europe

One of the great unanticipated benefits of European integration has been its role in improving the protection of the environment. This was not an idea that occurred to many Europeans or their leaders at the time that the precursors to the EU were being designed and built, but it later became clear that one of the most troublesome barriers to the single market was different environmental standards. As more was learned, and western publics became more aware of the costs of environmental mismanagement, integration encouraged a coordinated and wide-ranging response. The result is that almost all environmental laws and policies in today's Europe bear the hallmark of EU initiatives. Water and air are cleaner, there are tighter controls

over the production and management of waste, the health of
Europeans has been better protected against radiation and radioac-
tivity, Europe today has the world's tightest regimen for the management and control of chemicals and pesticides, the EU is a world
leader in promoting green energy, the control of genetically modified
organisms and the promotion of organic agriculture have both
moved high up the policy agenda, wildlife and natural habitats are
better protected, and – thanks to an expanded body of laws on noise
pollution – Europe is a quieter than it once was.

On almost every comparative indicator, from the consumption of
energy to the production of waste and pollution, the EU performs
better than almost any other part of the developed world. This is not
only good for Europeans, but it also gives the EU advantages that
increase its influence as a promoter of more sensible and sustainable
environmental policies on a global scale. That the Scandinavians and
the Dutch have their own progressive domestic targets on environmental policy is well known, but the dynamics of European integration have allowed the influence of those targets to be felt in eastern
Europe, Russia and even further afield in a way that could never
have been achieved by individual western European states working
alone.

7: Raising Standards and Expectations

Some of the most impressive achievements of European integration
have grown out of peer pressure. Independent states can improve
their policy performance by learning from the records of others, but
involvement in a communal exercise like regional integration alters
the pace and the reach of change. The leaders – states with higher
standards and greater ambitions – set the pace, obliging laggards to
make changes in order to remove barriers to the achievement of the
common goals of the group. The pressures have led to a race to the
top rather than a dive to the bottom.

There are numerous examples where initiatives in leader states have
brought change in laggard states that would probably never otherwise
have happened, or at least would have taken much longer: these
include health and safety standards, environmental policy, financial
regulation, entrepreneurial opportunity, education, technology and

consumer policy. The story of eastern Europe's transition to democracy and capitalism would also have taken longer to unfold without such pressures; in many cases, entire bodies of law were missing from the statute books of those countries, and have only been inserted as part of the requirement of EU membership. And this has meant benefits also for more progressive states, which have not been threatened by the economic imbalances that would have accrued from having less progressive states on their doorstep.

And the effects do not end at the borders of the EU. Thanks to their combined political and economic reach, the states of the EU have been able to exert an influence over other parts of the world to an extent that none of them working alone would have been able to achieve. They have been in a stronger position to make demands on issues as varied as human rights, climate change, capital punishment, development aid, and the promotion of democracy. There is no guarantee that laggard states within the EU will keep up with the leaders, or that the EU's international influence will succeed, but the pressures for change are greater when the EU works in concert.

8: Building a World-class Single Currency

To describe the euro as a world-class currency against the background of its recent problems might be to risk having readers rubbing their eyes in disbelief. But while we have had plenty of reminders of its problems, let us pause for a moment and recollect the many benefits of a single currency: cross-border travel without the need to exchange currencies, greater transparency that allows consumers to compare prices, lowered transaction costs, less concern about the risks posed by fluctuations in exchange rates, improved opportunities for exports and investment, a bigger market for businesses without concerns about currency exchanges and transaction costs, the psychological advantages of the foreign being more familiar, and the provision of a world-class currency with political and economic benefits for Europe. The Deutschmark and the French franc might well have been world-class currencies, as is the British pound today, but they came nowhere close to providing Europe with the global monetary influence that comes with a single currency.

We should also remember that prior to the breaking of the euro zone crisis, there was sustained public support for the euro, and even speculation that it might replace the US dollar as the world's preferred reserve currency, with all the political and economic influence that this would entail. It will take time to rebuild these levels of optimism and confidence, and the reorganization of the euro will mean the surrender of more national controls to the European Central Bank and a cluster of financial agencies. But the benefits of a single currency will continue indefinitely to outweigh its costs, and a revived and redesigned euro will have the additional advantage of being managed by governments and policymakers that have gone through a steep learning curve and developed a better grasp of its limitations and possibilities.

9: Promoting Democracy and Free Markets at Home and Abroad

European integration has not just brought lasting peace at home but has also been a critical force in the promotion of democracy and free markets more widely. Cooperation helped avert the political drift to the far left after 1945, encouraged stability among the six founding members of the EEC, and both accelerated and provided incentives for the transition to democracy and free markets in newer states. The original informal terms of EEC membership were based on the assumption that only states with open and stable societies would be allowed to join, but the formal terms of membership today require that new members must be democratic and capitalist, as well as being able to adopt the existing body of EU laws and policies.

The close and circular relationship between open government and open markets has combined with the new economic opportunities made available by integration to strengthen the democratic and free market records of the older EU member states, to accelerate change in newer eastern European states, and to encourage change in non-EU countries that have hopes of joining the club, or even in non-European states that seek access to the European market. Such changes are good for all involved, but there are also broader implications: the EU is proof of the political and economic benefits of free

Box 17: Twenty reasons why Europe matters

1. Replacing self-interest with shared interests.
2. Adapting to changes in the international system.
3. Bringing a lasting peace to Europe.
4. Offering a benchmark model of civilian power.
5. Bringing prosperity, innovation, opportunity and choice.
6. Promoting a cleaner and greener Europe.
7. Raising standards and expectations.
8. Building a world-class single currency.
9. Promoting democracy and free markets at home and abroad.
10. Strengthening human rights at home and abroad.
11. Stimulating a European identity.
12. Replacing exclusion with inclusion.
13. Helping Europeans understand their shared values.
14. Encouraging cooperation and efficiency.
15. Reducing regulation and red tape.
16. Offering an example to the rest of the world.
17. Allowing Europe to speak with a louder voice
18. Encouraging a rules-based approach to international affairs.
19. Sustaining the world's largest trading bloc.
20. Strengthening the corporate reach of Europe.

trade, and as much of the rest of the world engages in its own separate integrative projects, the pressures for democratic and free market change expand.

We should also not forget that the process of European integration itself involves a greater degree of democracy and responsiveness than its critics suggest. True, elites have been at the heart of the design and development of the EU, and many of its key initiatives have not been put to the test of public opinion. But polls reveal that those who support the EU outnumber those who do not, and there are multiple channels though which the interests of Europeans are protected and through which their views can be expressed (or indirectly represented). That many have failed to exploit these opportunities does not mean that there is a crisis of legitimacy in the EU.

10: Strengthening Human Rights at Home and Abroad

The leader–laggard dynamic has had some of its most impressive results in the field of human rights, where standards and expectations have improved as a result of efforts by European states to develop a common set of measures of essential rights, and to ensure their protection and promotion. This is also one area where Europe means more than the EU: the baseline for the strengthening of human rights was provided by the 1953 European Convention on Human Rights, a brainchild of the Council of Europe. More standards were established in 2000 by the Charter of Fundamental Rights of the European Union. Both documents set targets not just for existing participants in the European project but also for aspirants, and the work of the European Court of Human Rights gave the 1953 convention more substance by providing a forum in which the abuse of human rights could be publicly challenged.

Most western European states already had strong records on human rights prior to 1953, but by developing these shared agreements, they brought peer pressure to bear and ensured that expectations were exported to states with poorer records. The effect has been to provide common targets and to raise expectations, thereby helping strengthen the democratic record of almost all European states in a manner that would have taken longer and proceeded quite differently without this communal approach. And Europe has gone further by using its combined weight to push for human rights reforms in other parts of the world, in a way that not even the biggest and most powerful European states working in isolation would have been able to emulate.

11: Stimulating a European Identity

The identification of Europeans with nations and states has been behind many of the region's most difficult stresses and conflicts, has often led to war, and remains a problem today as many Europeans continue to adhere to the kind of exclusionary views that often arise when people define themselves by political frontiers and cultural barriers. While integration has involved a degree of homogenization, and in this sense has created some of the challenges to national identity that eurosceptics bemoan, the advantages have far outweighed the cost. As the ties of Europeans to states diminish, so the indications of state identity fade away and people focus more on what unites them rather than what divides them.

Rather than creating some kind of awful and drab eurocitizen, European integration has instead removed the kinds of petty and annoying barriers that have for so long kept Europeans apart, while allowing them to retain almost everything of value that makes them different and to celebrate their diversity, whether it is language, culture, national symbols, cuisine or social norms. And national identity has grown in parallel with integration, so that Europeans are working more closely together at the continental level while also reasserting – in a mainly benign and non-threatening fashion – their national differences at the local level. The sense that they are all involved in a shared project with beneficial outcomes has grown; polls have found that about 60 per cent of Europeans feel some sense of belonging to Europe while also retaining some of their national and local identities.

12: Replacing Exclusion with Inclusion

One of the great achievements of Europe has been to help redefine the meaning of two ideas that have long been the most troubling consequence of states: citizenship and patriotism. The former provides helpful legal and political order, and the latter can provide a reassuring sense of belonging, but taken too far they both promote a sense of superiority, exceptionalism and parochialism. When the legal functionality of citizenship spills over into a belligerent defence of 'national interests', and patriotism is manipulated in order to whip up resentment against other states or to encourage a sense of superiority and exclusivity, we start sailing into stormy waters.

Integration has helped move Europeans away from an exclusive pride in the interests and symbols of the state and towards a pride in the kinds of ideas that unite rather than divide us. Where once many Europeans regarded each other as foreign and exotic, and with mistrust and suspicion, they now mainly regard each other as neighbours and partners, tied by overlapping sets of values and ideas. By giving Europeans the opportunity to travel more freely, to interact more easily with their counterparts in neighbouring states, and to share ideas, the EU has helped promote multiculturalism. Europe has long been a continent of migrants, but the opening of borders has given them more frequent and direct experience of their neighbours, further dissolving the barriers that once encouraged distrust and misunderstanding. (When it comes to racial and religious tolerance, however, the European record has not been good.)

13: Helping Europeans Understand Their Shared Values

Where the history of Europe before 1945 was driven by the differences among its governments and peoples, its modern history has been driven more by what they have in common and by the values that they share. European integration has both built on this new realization and been its primary champion. One of its great achievements has been to discourage hostility, discrimination and conflict, and to help bridge many of Europe's divisions by helping Europeans better appreciate their similarities. Increasingly, the values and interests of communities, nations and states have coalesced to become the values and interests of Europe.

Prime among the explanations for this has been the habit of consensual decision making required by integration. Most states are inclined to pursue narrow self-interest, which can lead to insularity, tensions and occasionally to war. But European integration has obliged governments and people to work together and to consider a wider array of explanations and solutions for problems, and a broader range of interests and perspectives. Bringing more minds to bear on a problem may slow down decision making, but it can also promote habits of cooperation, which can in turn remind us that we are often not all that different.

Yes, we all know the jokes and the stereotypes that Europeans like to share about each other, but all it often takes is for Europeans to travel outside Europe to better appreciate how much they think and act like those neighbours. Many of the qualities that are today so distinctively European – including support for the welfare state, multiculturalism, community rights, secularism, peace, cosmopolitanism and multilateralism – have long been there to different degrees, but they would not have evolved in quite the same way without the bridges offered by European integration.

14: Encouraging Cooperation and Efficiency

States that look inward will be more likely to draw only on the resources and expertise available within their borders. Thus they will be less likely to learn from the achievements and mistakes of others, will often duplicate the work of others, and will have less access to the experience and networks of others. The European project has helped address these problems, not only by pooling decision making in shared or common areas of policy, but also by pooling talent and knowledge.

Each of the member states brings its own strengths to the meeting rooms of the EU. Those strengths might be greater wealth, greater unmet economic possibilities, new ideas about how to address pressing policy issues, better links with governments in other parts of the world, or corporate creativity and productivity. They also – it must be said – bring their own weaknesses to those meeting rooms, whether in the form of greater poverty, a lack of progress in dealing with political problems, incomplete and confused foreign policies, nationalism, or underperforming economic sectors. But by pooling knowledge and transferring resources, the more successful ideas can be exported and replicated, and states suffering problems can draw on the experience of others.

To affiliate the terms 'Europe' and 'efficiency' is to fly in the face of some of the most common criticisms of European institutions and decision-making procedures. But while they are certainly imperfect, one of the core effects of integration has been to brush aside the detritus of obstruction, protection, self-interest and centuries-long records of European states developing separate and conflicting standards. Where are the benefits, for example, in different systems of weights and measures, different standards on consumer health and safety, different procedures for buying homes, or – the bane of the international traveller – different designs for electrical plugs and outlets? Many of these differences can and have been removed without threats to national identity and with the benefit of greater efficiency and higher standards.

15: Reducing Regulation and Red Tape

One of the longest-enduring myths about the European project is that it has imposed new regulatory burdens on Europe, and is a source of red tape that limits rather than expands options for Europeans. But every law generated by the EU legislative process came out of the requirements of treaties and out of policies agreed by the governments of the member states, and went through a rigorous and often lengthy process of drafting and approval involving national governments and multiple interested parties before being enacted. And the existence of European institutions has allowed these laws to be drafted and discussed in a relatively straightforward manner by institutions representing several different levels of public interest, where otherwise progress would have been determined on the basis of treaties negotiated by governments, with little or no democratic input.

The development of these new laws has resulted in improved standards and more ambitious goals, but it has also resulted in the removal of national laws that would otherwise have remained a handicap to the single market, has harmonized national laws so that Europeans enjoy the same standards and rights wherever they travel within the EU, and in many cases has reduced the regulatory burden on Europeans. As we have seen, the exact number of European laws active at any given time is hard to know, and the number of national laws that are adopted as part of the requirement of European laws is even harder to know, but most popular estimates of the EU legal 'burden' are grossly inflated. And while there are certainly examples of European laws that make one wonder what their authors were thinking, the same is also true at the state and local level, and a modicum of absurdity should not make us lose sight of the vastly greater number of European laws that have been entirely sensible and have made life better for all concerned.

16: Offering an Example to the Rest of the World

If European integration is the flawed notion that so many of its critics suggest, then it is reasonable to ask why so many other parts of the world are engaged in their own parallel initiatives. In spite of the many wrong turnings in the building of the European project, it has clearly occurred to a great many other people and governments that regional integration has something to offer in terms of new opportunities and efficiencies. In Africa, Asia and the Americas there are multiple examples of integration at the regional, subcontinental and continental level, ranging in scope from free trade agreements to customs unions, monetary unions and single markets. The countries involved may not be copying the European template exactly, and in some cases may be learning as much from Europe's mistakes as from its achievements, but the broader argument holds true: Europe has shown that regional integration offers political and economic benefits that in many areas outweigh the standard approaches of states.

17: Allowing Europe to Speak with a Louder Voice

The great world powers were once almost all European, but that era ended with the shock of the Second World War and the end of empire. Europe celebrated peace in April 1945 but also found itself internally divided and subject for the first time in its history to the lead of external powers, a problem that would later contribute to efforts to build regional integration. By the time the cold war ended and the world entered the brief era of American hegemony in the 1990s, the EU was well on its way to building the connections that would allow it to develop common foreign, security and defence policies. The results have been mixed, to be sure, but in a world where the balance of power and influence is changing so rapidly, and where the population of Europe is declining in relative terms, the EU is the most effective tool that Europeans have available to make themselves heard in the meeting rooms of international organizations.

It is easy to remember how often the EU has faced a crisis of leadership, or has failed to offer answers to critical international questions, but the governments of its member states would have been all but ignored but for the channels of cooperation that have been made available through integration. And just because the EU can some-times be overlooked in the debates over international issues, this does not mean that it has not made its mark. Cooperation has helped EU member states use their combined influence, allowed smaller EU states to take part in large international debates, combines the skills and resources of multiple countries, and encourages the pooling and sharing of ideas while minimizing duplication.

And while it is also easy to criticize the EU for its failure to develop a single defence policy and to step up to the plate on many critical international conflicts, we should remember that the EU was never intended to be a military actor. On the contrary, the sheer success of its efforts to encourage peace at home, built on a founda-tion of economic cooperation and opportunity, have moulded the EU into a global actor like no other: one that prefers diplomacy and cooperation to violence and coercion. It is unlikely that such a philosophy would have emerged without the incentives offered by integration.

18: Encouraging a Rules-based Approach to International Affairs

Thanks to the habits of cooperation and consensus that Europeans have developed under the auspices of the EU, they have become global champions of efforts to take more coordinated approaches to the definition and solution of international problems. The dangers of global or regional hegemons placing their self-interest above broader regional or even global interests are well known, and while such hegemons are adept at offering leadership, the directions in which they take us are not always in the communal interest. History has also shown that while a great power can dream about moulding the world in its image and according to its perceptions, none has ever succeeded and nor should it. Far better that we take a cooperative and multilateral view based on rules and building a consensus, and in this regard there are few better examples of success than the European Union.

The member states of the EU have had decades of experience of consensus building based on the merging of competing interests and agendas. And while achieving a consensus can take time, inevitably waters down goals, demands compromises, often delays action, and ensures that no one will get exactly what they want, it also helps us rise above the narrow and the insular (qualities which regrettably still feature in American, Chinese and Russian calculations) to embrace the broad and universal. And as a means of making decisions on a regional or global scale in today's political and economic environment, consensus is the only workable option.

19: Sustaining the World's Largest Trading Bloc

Strangely overlooked in most assessments of the EU have been its achievements on the trading front. Building a common trade policy was one of the original goals of the Treaty of Rome, but while the single market was famously focused on bringing down internal trade barriers, less attention was paid to European prospects at a global scale. And yet the European project has been highly effective in first reaching agreement among its member states, and then having a single European representative – the commissioner for trade – negotiate with third parties on behalf of the entire EU. And since the EU is the wealthiest marketplace in the world, accounting for the biggest shares of trade in goods and services, this is a voice to which everyone pays close attention.

The EU has not always had its own way, and it has irritated its trading partners with practices that run counter to international agreements and the principles of the World Trade Organization (WTO), but it has been the leading exponent and example of the benefits of free trade. Open economies grow faster than those that retain restrictions, creating new jobs and opportunities, encouraging efficiency and innovation, and making more and better goods and services available to consumers at lower prices. And the combined power of the member states of the EU has been effectively wielded to help them exert influence over the global trading system, pursuing its key goals of competition, investment, free trade, and access to government contracts.

Little of this could have been done without the EU. Even the biggest EU economies – Germany, France, Britain and Italy – are, by themselves, much smaller than the United States, China and Japan, and if they had separate seats around the negotiating tables of the

WTO, they would be treated accordingly. But by working together, they transform themselves into one of the two giants in the room (the United States being the second), and they promote efficiency by reaching prior agreements among themselves that they then bring to the negotiations.

20: Strengthening the Corporate Reach of Europe

One of the effects of the Second World War was for European businesses to lose ground first to American and then to Japanese competition. While the Americans and the Japanese were daring, aggressive and dynamic, European companies were conservative, nationalistic and modest, their prospects limited by a fragmented local marketplace where efforts to cross borders were hobbled by different regulations and standards, discriminatory taxes, and limits on the movement of capital, goods and services. Even today, the United States remains far ahead of Europe in maintaining the conditions that spawn new and innovative companies such as Google and Amazon.

But much has changed, and where European companies once preferred to acquire or merge with other companies in the same country, or those outside Europe, the single market has sparked a growth in the number of cross-border mergers and acquisitions within the EU. This has created large European companies that are better able to compete in the global marketplace, and that are better placed to create new jobs, generate new investments, explore new ideas, spread risk, and exploit differences in labour markets. They do not always behave as politely as we might hope, and there are plenty of examples of European multinationals engaging in exploitation and in activities of questionable ethical merit, but this has always been the way in the cut-throat world of international commerce. And better that Europe join the Americans and the Japanese in wielding the kind of soft power that corporations often represent, and in weaving the kinds of economic and financial webs that discourage conflict and war.

Here, then, we have 20 reasons why Europe matters, and why the European Union deserves our support. Europe is a brave and laudable endeavour, which has brought real and tangible benefits, making the lives of Europeans safer, more peaceful and more prosperous. As we have seen, there has been too little engagement with Europe by ordinary Europeans, leaving many of the decisions about the direction it has taken in the hands of elites, and making the European project seem distant and opaque. But this need not always be so. The time is ripe for change, and it will only be with better engagement and closer understanding that we will have a more constructive debate about Europe, allowing us to move it in the direction that brings the greatest benefits in the shortest time to the most people at the lowest cost.

Notes

Preface

1. Hubert Zimmermann and Andreas Dür (eds), *Key Controversies in European Integration* (Basingstoke: Palgrave Macmillan, 2012).

Introduction

1. European Commission, *Eurobarometer* 75 (Spring 2011), 46, 61.
2. European Commission, *Eurobarometer* 77 (Spring 2012), First Results, 19.
3. *The Economist*, 'Alas, Poor Europe', 20 March 1982, 11.
4. José Manuel Barroso, 'Speaking with One Voice: Defining and Defending the European Interest'. Speech to the European Parliament, Strasbourg, 9 February 2010.
5. Andrew Duff, *Federal Union Now* (London: The Federal Trust, 2011).
6. While hardly scientific, a search for 'European Union' and 'conspiracy' on Google in October 2012 generated nearly 7.4 million hits.
7. Paul Taggart and Aleks Szczerbiak, 'Parties, Positions and Europe: Euroscepticism in the Candidate States of Central and Eastern Europe'. Paper presented at the Annual Meeting of the Political Studies Association, Manchester, April 2001.
8. Petr Kopecký and Cas Mudde, 'The Two Sides of Euroscepticism: Party Positions on European Integration in East Central Europe', *European Union Politics* 3:3 (September 2002), 297–326.
9. Robert Harmsen and Menno Spiering, 'Introduction: Euroscepticism and the Evolution of European Political Debate', in Robert Harmsen and Menno Spiering (eds), *Euroscepticism: Party Politics, National Identity and European Integration* (Amsterdam: Rodopi, 2004), 15–16.
10. Jean-Marie Le Pen, *L'Espoir* (Paris: Editions Albatross, 1989), 366–7.
11. See Klaus Busch and Wilhelm Knelangen, 'German Euroscepticism', in Robert Harmsen and Menno Spiering (eds), *Euroscepticism: Party Politics, National Identity and European Integration* (Amsterdam: Rodopi, 2004).
12. See, for example, Joseph Schumpeter, *Capitalism, Socialism, and Democracy* (New York: Harper & Row, 1950); Anthony Downs, *An Economic Theory of Democracy* (New York: Harper and Row, 1957); W. Russell Neuman, *The Paradox of Mass Publics: Knowledge and Opinion in the American Electorate* (Cambridge, MA: Harvard University Press, 1986); and Philip E. Converse, 'Assessing the Capacity of Mass Electorates', *Annual Review of Political Science* 3 (June 2000), 331–53.

13. See Arthur Lupia, 'Busy Voters, Agenda Control, and the Power of Information', *American Political Science Review* 86:2 (1992), 390–404, and Richard R. Lau and David P. Redlwask, *How Voters Decide: Information Processing During Election Campaigns* (New York: Cambridge University Press, 2006).

14. See Philip E. Tetlock, *Expert Political Judgment: How Good Is It? How Can We Know?* (Princeton, NJ: Princeton University Press, 2005).

15. Nate Silver, *The Signal and the Noise: Why Most Predictions Fail but Some Don't* (New York: Penguin, 2012).

16. Martin Feldstein, 'The Failure of the Euro', *Foreign Affairs* 91:1 (January/February 2012), 105–16.

17. C. Fred Bergsten, 'Why the Euro Will Survive', *Foreign Affairs* 91:5 (September/October 2012), 16–22.

1 What Is Europe?

1. Jean Monnet, *Memoirs* (Garden City, NY: Doubleday, 1978), 417.

2. Ibid., 109.

3. See Thomas Wright, 'What if Europe Fails?' *Washington Quarterly* 35:3 (Summer 2012), 23–41, and Steven Philip Kramer, 'The Return of History in Europe', *Washington Quarterly* 35:4 (Fall 2012), 81–91.

4. Susan Strange, *The Retreat of the State: The Diffusion of Power in the World Economy* (Cambridge: Cambridge University Press, 1996), 4.

5. BBC Online, 'Nigel Farage: UK Election Outcomes Irrelevant, Because of EU', 2 August 2012.

6. Milton Friedman, in introduction to Leonard E. Read, 'I, Pencil' (Irvington-on-Hudson, NY: The Foundation for Economic Education, 1999).

7. *The Economist*, 'Beyond the Fringe', 12 November 2011.

8. *New York Times*, 'EU Elites Keep Power from the People', 22 August 2011.

9. See Charles Handy, *Understanding Organizations*, 4th edn (Harlow: Penguin Global, 2005); Howard Lune, *Understanding Organizations* (Oxford: Polity Press, 2011); Stephen P. Robbins and Timothy A. Judge, *Organizational Behavior*, 15th edn (Upper Saddle River, NJ: Prentice Hall, 2012).

10. Simon Hix, *What's Wrong with the European Union and How to Fix It* (Cambridge: Polity, 2008), 51.

11. 'Arguments against the EU'. Factsheet dated 27 July 2011 at www.civitas. org.uk/eufacts (accessed July 2012).

12. Jonathan Powell, 'Out of Europe, Britain Faces a Weak Future', *Financial Times*, 11 December 2012.

13. Office for National Statistics, UK, at www.ons.gov.uk (accessed February 2012). Figure is for third quarter, 2011.

14. Figures for 2010 from European Commission, *EU Budget 2010 – Financial Report* (Luxembourg, 2011), 53.

15. Figures derived or calculated from National Health Service (2012) at www.nhs.uk. See also *The Guardian*, 29 March 2010, 'NHS spends 14% of budget on management, MPs reveal'.

16. William Wallace, 'Europe as a Confederation: the Community and the Nation-State', *Journal of Common Market Studies* 21:1 (1982), 57–68.

17. Giandomenico Majone, 'Federation, Confederation, and Mixed Government: An EU–US Comparison', in Anand Menon and Martin Schain

(eds), *Comparative Federalism: The European Union and the United States in Comparative Perspective* (Oxford: Oxford University Press, 2006), 136.

18. Andrew Moravcsik, 'The European Constitutional Settlement', in Sophie Meunier and Kathleen R. McNamara (eds), *Making History: European Integration and Institutional Change at Fifty* (Oxford: Oxford University Press, 2007), 25.

19. *The Economist*, 'Wake up Europe!', 10–16 October 2009.

20. José Manuel Barroso, State of the Union Address, delivered to the European Parliament, 12 September 2012.

21. Frederick K. Lister, *The European Union, the United Nations, and the Revival of Confederal Governance* (Westport, CT: Greenwood, 1996), 106.

22. Donald J. Puchala, 'Domestic Politics and Regional Harmonization in the European Communities', *World Politics* 27:4 (July 1975), 496–520; Gary Marks, 'Structural Policy and Multi-level Governance in the EC', in Alan Cafruny and Glenda Rosenthal (eds), *The State of the European Community*, vol. 2 (Boulder, CO: Lynne Rienner, 1993); Liesbet Hooghe and Gary Marks, *Multi-Level Governance and European Integration* (Lanham, MD: Rowman and Littlefield, 2001).

23. Pascaline Winand, *Eisenhower, Kennedy and the United States of Europe* (New York: St Martin's Press, 1993), 257.

2 Europe as a Peacemaker

1. See discussion in Michael Howard, *The Invention of Peace: Reflections on War and International Order* (London: Profile Books, 2000).

2. Umberto Eco, 'It's Culture, Not War, That Cements European Identity', *The Guardian*, 26 January 2012 at www.guardian.co.uk/world/2012/jan/26/umberto-eco-culture-war-europa (last accessed 21 December 2012).

3. Timothy Garton Ash, 'The Crisis of Europe', *Foreign Affairs* 91:5 (September/October 2012), 2–15.

4. Gareth Harding, 'Public support for the EU is falling. Here are 10 tips for the pro-EU crowd to get the EU back on track', on London School of Economics blog at http://blogs.lse.ac.uk/europpblog (posted 12 March 2012).

5. See discussion in John R. Oneal and Bruce Russett, 'The Kantian Peace: The Pacific Benefits of Democracy, Interdependence, and International Organizations, 1885–1992' *World Politics* 52:1 (1999), 1–37.

6. Geoffrey Blainey, *The Causes of War*, 3rd edn (New York: Free Press, 1988), 3.

7. Kenneth N. Waltz, 'Structural Realism after the Cold War', *International Security* 25:1 (Summer 2000), 5–41.

8. See Jack S. Levy, 'The Causes of War: A Review of Theories and Evidence', in Philip E. Tetlock et al. (eds), *Behavior, Society and Nuclear War*, vol. 1 (New York: Oxford University Press, 1989).

9. Human Security Report Project, *Human Security Report 2009–10: The Causes of Peace and the Shrinking Costs of War* (New York: Oxford University Press, 2011).

10. John J. Mearsheimer, 'Why Is Europe Peaceful Today?' *European Political Science* 9:3 (September 2010), 387–97.

11. David Mitrany, *A Working Peace System* (Chicago: Quadrangle, 1966).

12. See Sanford Gottlieb, *Defense Addiction; Can America Kick the Habit?* (Boulder, CO: Westview Press, 1997); James Ledbetter, *Unwarranted*

Influence: Dwight D. Eisenhower and the Military-Industrial Complex (New Haven: Yale University Press, 2011); and Adrian R. Lewis, *The American Culture of War: The History of US Military Force from World War II to Operation Enduring Freedom*, 2nd edn (New York: Routledge, 2012).

13. George Soros, Remarks at the Festival of Economics, Trento, Italy (2 June 2012), at www.georgesoros.com.

14. 'The Sociology of Imperialism', reproduced in Joseph Schumpeter, *Imperialism and Social Classes* (Cleveland, OH: World Publishing, 1955), 68.

15. See discussion in Michael W. Doyle, *Ways of War and Peace* (New York: W. W. Norton, 1997).

16. Thomas L. Friedman, *The Lexus and the Olive Tree* (New York: Farrar, Straus & Giroux, 1999).

17. See, for example, John R. Oneal and Bruce Russett, 'The Kantian Peace: The Pacific Benefits of Democracy, Interdependence, and International Organizations, 1885–1992', *World Politics* 52:1 (October 1999), 1–37.

18. Michael Howard, *The Causes of War and Other Essays*, 2nd edn (Cambridge: Harvard University Press, 1983), 245.

19. Christopher Storrs (ed.), *The Fiscal-Military State in Eighteenth-Century Europe* (Farnham: Ashgate, 2009).

20. US Department of Defense, *Base Structure Report* (Washington, DC: US Department of Defense, 2009), 22.

21. Stockholm International Peace Research Institute, *SIPRI Yearbook 2011: Armaments, Disarmament and International Security* (Oxford: Oxford University Press, 2011).

22. See Minxin Pei, 'Lessons From the Past: The American Record on Nation-Building', Carnegie Endowment Policy Brief No. 24, April 2003, and Bruce Bueno de Mesquita and George W. Downs, 'Why Gun-Barrel Democracy Doesn't Work', *Hoover Digest* 2 (Spring 2004).

23. Human Security Report Project, *Human Security Report 2009–10: The Causes of Peace and the Shrinking Costs of War* (New York: Oxford University Press, 2011).

24. Anne-Marie Slaughter, 'War and Law in the 21st Century: Adapting to the Changing Face of Conflict', *Europe's World* 19 (Autumn 2011), 32–7.

25. International Institute for Strategic Studies, *The Military Balance 2011*, vol. 111, no. 1 (2011).

26. Karen E. Smith, 'Still "Civilian Power EU"?', European Foreign Policy Unit Working Paper 2005/1 (2005).

27. Martin Shaw, *Post-Military Society: Militarism, Demilitarization and War at the End of the Twentieth Century* (Philadelphia: Temple University Press, 1991), 11–13.

28. Maull, 'Germany and Japan', 91–106.

29. Joseph S. Nye, 'Soft Power', *Foreign Policy* 80 (Fall 1990), 153–72; Joseph S. Nye, *Bound to Lead: The Changing Nature of American Power* (New York: Basic Books, 1991); Joseph S. Nye, *Soft Power: The Means to Success in World Politics* (New York: Public Affairs, 2004), 5–7.

30. See discussion in John Gerard Ruggie, 'Multilateralism: The Anatomy of an Institution', *International Organization* 46:3 (Summer 1992), 561–98; John Gerard Ruggie (ed.), *Multilateralism Matters: The Theory and Praxis of an Institutional Form* (New York: Columbia University Press, 1993).

31. Andrew J. Bacevich (2005), *The New American Militarism: How Americans are Seduced by War* (New York: Oxford University Press).

32. James J. Sheehan, *Where Have All the Soldiers Gone? The Transformation of Modern Europe* (Boston: Houghton Mifflin, 2008), 174–5.
33. Anthony Sampson (1968) *The New Europeans: A Guide to the Workings, Institutions, and Character of Contemporary Western Europe* (London: Hodder and Stoughton), 207.
34. François Duchêne, 'Europe's Role in World Peace', in Richard Mayne (ed.), *Europe Tomorrow: Sixteen Europeans Look Ahead* (London: Fontana, 1972), 43, 47.
35. François Duchêne, 'The European Community and the Uncertainties of Interdependence', in Max Kohnstamm and Wolfgang Hager (eds), *A Nation Writ Large? Foreign Policy Problems Before the European Community* (London: Macmillan, 1973).
36. Bacevich, *The New American Militarism*, xii.
37. Quoted by Mearsheimer, 'Why Is Europe Peaceful Today?', 387–97.
38. US Defense Secretary Robert Gates, reported by Associated Press, 23 February 2010.

3 Europe as a Marketplace

1. German Marshall Fund, *Transatlantic Trends* (Washington, DC: German Marshall Fund, 2011), 19. Based on surveys taken in May–June 2011 in Bulgaria, France, Germany, Italy, the Netherlands, Poland, Portugal, Romania, Slovakia, Spain, Sweden, Turkey and the UK.
2. *The Economist*, 'Unity Is Strength', 10 March 2012.
3. *The Economist*, 'Coming off the Rails', 20 October 2012.
4. *The Economist*, 'It'll Cost You', 14 April 2012.
5. BusinessEurope, 'Unleashing Cross-Border Services', January 2011.
6. Council of the European Union, Final Report of the Committee of Wise Men on the Regulation of the European Securities Markets (chaired by Alexandre Lamfalussy). Brussels, 15 February 2001.
7. Ann Mettler and Sylwia Stępień (2012), 'Why European SMEs Need the Digital Single Market', on EurActiv at www.euractiv.com (accessed 23 April 2012).
8. Hans Martens and Fabian Zuleeg, 'The Digital Single Market 2.0'. Policy Brief, European Policy Centre, 27 February 2012.
9. *The Economist*, 'Briefing: European Entrepreneurs', 28 July 2012.
10. Thomas Philippon and Nicolas Véron, 'Financing Europe's Fast Movers', Policy Brief 2008/01, January 2008, Bruegel, Brussels.
11. Quoted in *Financial Times*, 'Rebel Seeks Innovators to Shake up Europe', 15 January 2008.
12. European Commission, *Eurobarometer* 73 (Spring 2010), 204.
13. Copenhagen Economics, *Eco-Innovation and Resource Efficiency: Gains from Reforms*. Report for the European Policy Centre, October 2011, available at www.epc.eu.
14. Herbert Giersch, *Eurosclerosis* (Kiel: Institut für Weltwirtschaft, 1985).
15. Joschka Fischer, 'From Confederacy to Federation: Thoughts on the Finality of European Integration', speech given at Humboldt University, Berlin, 12 May 2000.
16. European Commission, *Eurobarometer* 77 (Spring 2012), First Results, 15, 20.

17. German Marshall Fund, *Transatlantic Trends*, 19.
18. Economist Intelligence Unit, *State of the Union: Can the Euro Zone Survive Its Debt Crisis?* (London: Economist Intelligence Unit, 2011), 4.

4 Europe as a Democracy

1. Credited to Lord Dahrendorf. See debate on European Communities (Amendment) Bill, 28 January 2002. Hansard Vol. 631, cc. 26–36. Also credited to David Martin, quoted in Vernon Bogdanor and Geoffrey Woodcock, 'The European Community and Sovereignty', *Parliamentary Affairs* 44:4 (October 1991), 481–92.
2. Andrew Moravcsik, 'In Defence of the "Democratic Deficit": Reassessing Legitimacy in the European Union', *Journal of Common Market Studies* 40:4 (November 2002), 603–24.
3. European Commission, *Eurobarometer* 77 (Spring 2012), First Results, 14.
4. European Commission, *Eurobarometer* 74 (Autumn 2010), 48.
5. European Commission, *Eurobarometer* 75 (Spring 2011), 43.
6. European Commission, *Eurobarometer* 77 (Spring 2012), First Results, 13.
7. European Commission, *Eurobarometer* 75 (Autumn 2011), 30.
8. See, for example, Rasmussen Reports 9–15 July 2012 on Newsmax at www.newsmax.com.
9. European Commission, *Eurobarometer* 75 (Spring 2011), 55.
10. European Commission, *Eurobarometer* 75 (Spring 2011), 61.
11. European Commission, *Eurobarometer* 63 (September 2005), 75.
12. European Commission, *Eurobarometer* 74 (Autumn 2010), 13; European Commission, *Eurobarometer* 76 (Autumn 2011), 72.
13. European Commission, *Eurobarometer* 67 (November 2007), 131, and European Commission, *Eurobarometer* 75 (Spring 2011), 49.
14. European Commission, *Eurobarometer* 68 (May 2008), 158, and European Commission, *Eurobarometer* 75 (Spring 2011), 49.
15. *Flash Eurobarometer*: Attitudes towards the EU in the United Kingdom, July 2009.
16. See, for example, Paul M. Sniderman, Richard A. Brody and Philip E. Tetlock, *Reasoning and Choice: Explorations in Political Psychology* (New York: Cambridge University Press, 1991); Benjamin I. Page and Robert Y. Shapiro, *The Rational Public: Fifty Years of Trends in Americans' Policy Preferences* (Chicago: University of Chicago Press, 1992); and Samuel L. Popkin, *The Reasoning Voter: Communication and Persuasion in Presidential Campaigns* (Chicago: University of Chicago Press, 1994).
17. Nate Silver, *The Signal and the Noise: Why Most Predictions Fail but Some Don't* (New York: Penguin, 2012).
18. Cass Sunstein, *Echo Chambers: Bush v. Gore, Impeachment, and Beyond* (Princeton: Princeton University Press, 2001), 2.
19. For discussion, see Mark Franklin, 'European Elections and the European Voter', in Jeremy Richardson (ed.), *European Union: Power and Policy-Making*, 3rd edn (Abingdon: Routledge, 2006), and David Judge and David Earnshaw, *The European Parliament*, 2nd edn (Basingstoke: Palgrave Macmillan, 2008), 77–80.

20. European Commission, *Eurobarometer* 63 (Spring 2005), 138.
21. Gilles Ivaldi, 'Beyond France's 2005 Referendum on the European Constitutional Treaty', *West European Politics* 29:1 (2006), 47–69.
22. Richard Balme and Didier Chabanet, *European Governance and Democracy: Power and Protest in the EU* (Lanham, MD: Rowman and Littlefield, 2008).
23. Steven Greer, *The European Convention on Human Rights: Achievements, Problems and Prospects* (Cambridge: Cambridge University Press, 2006), 48–9.
24. Web site of the European Court of Human Rights at www.echr.coe.int (accessed June 2010). Figures are for judgments issued between 1998 and 2009.
25. Greer, *The European Convention on Human Rights: Achievements, Problems and Prospects*, 34–40.
26. *International Herald Tribune*, 'Britain vs. the European Court of Human Rights', 19 April 2012.

5 Europe as a Community

1. *Der Spiegel*, 'Britain Losing Allegiance to the EU', 15 October 2012.
2. Peter L. Berger, 'Reflections on the *Sociology of Religion* Today', *Sociology of Religion* 62:4 (Winter 2001), 443–54. See also Grace Davie, *Europe: The Exceptional Case. Parameters of Faith in the Modern World* (London: Darton, Longman and Todd, 2002).
3. See discussion in Jonathan White, 'The Common European Identity Is an Illusion', in Hubert Zimmermann and Andreas Dür (eds), *Key Controversies in European Integration* (Basingstoke: Palgrave Macmillan, 2012).
4. Umberto Eco, 'It's Culture, Not War, That Cements European Identity', *Guardian*, 26 January 2012 at www.guardian.co.uk/world/2012/jan/26/umberto-eco-culture-war-europa.
5. Steven Erlanger, 'Europe's Richer Regions Want Out', *New York Times*, 6 October 2012.
6. Igor Primoratz (ed.), *Patriotism* (New York: Humanity Books, 2002).
7. Václav Havel, Address to Members of the European Parliament, Strasbourg, 16 February 2000.
8. Neil Fligstein, *Euroclash: The EU, European Identity, and the Future of Europe* (Oxford: Oxford University Press, 2008), 250.
9. T. R. Reid, *The United States of Europe* (New York: Penguin, 2004), chap. 8.
10. Adrian Favell, *Eurostars and Eurocities: Free Movement and Mobility in an Integrating Europe* (Oxford: Blackwell, 2008).
11. Ron Griffiths, 'City/Culture Discourses: Evidence from the Competition to Select the European Capital of Culture', *European Planning Studies* 14:4 (2006). See also Kiran Patel (ed.), *The Cultural Politics of Europe: European Capitals of Culture and European Union since 1980* (Abingdon: Routledge, 2012).
12. Robert Palmer et al., *European Cities and Capitals of Culture* (Brussels: Palmer-Rae Associates, 2004).
13. For a full listing, see European Commission, DG for Agriculture and Rural Development at http://ec.europa.eu/agriculture/quality/index_en.htm.

14. Eco, 'It's Culture, Not War, That Cements European Identity'.

15. Heiko Walkenhorst, 'Explaining Change in EU Education Policy', *Journal of European Public Policy* 15:4 (June 2008), 567–87.

16. Jürgen Habermas and Jacques Derrida, 'February 15, or What Binds Europe Together: Plea for a Common Foreign Policy, Beginning in Core Europe', *Frankfurter Allgemeine Zeitung*, 31 May 2003. Reproduced in Daniel Levy, Max Pensky and John Torpey (eds), *Old Europe, New Europe, Core Europe* (London: Verso, 2005).

17. Clyde Prestowitz, *Rogue Nation: American Unilateralism and the Failure of Good Intentions* (New York: Basic Books, 2003), 236–7.

18. Jeremy Rifkin, *The European Dream: How Europe's Vision of the Future Is Quietly Eclipsing the American Dream* (New York: Jeremy P. Tarcher/Penguin, 2004), 3.

19. Steven Hill, *Europe's Promise: Why the European Way Is the Best Hope for an Insecure Age* (Berkeley: University of California Press, 2010).

20. For a more detailed assessment of these preferences and values, see John McCormick, *Europeanism* (Oxford: Oxford University Press, 2010).

21. *The Economist*, 'Hopeful or Hopeless?', 28 January 2012.

22. For more details, see Amitai Etzioni, *The Spirit of Community: Rights, Responsibilities and the Communitarian Agenda* (London: Fontana Press, 1995).

23. See Ulrich Beck, *The Cosmopolitan Vision* (Cambridge: Polity Press, 2006), and Ulrich Beck and Edgar Grande, *Cosmopolitan Europe* (Cambridge: Polity Press, 2007).

24. For a review of its core ideas and history, see Jan-Werner Müller, *Constitutional Patriotism* (Princeton: Princeton University Press, 2007), 16–21, 26ff.

6 Europe as a Model

1. European Commission, *Eurobarometer* 74 (Autumn 2010), 48.

2. Gevin Hewitt, 'Europe and Its Long Crisis', BBC News online, 19 October 2012, at www.bbc.co.uk/news.

3. Marco Brunazzo and Vincent Della Sella, 'A Good Idea That Lost Its Way; Cohesion Policy in the EU', in Hubert Zimmermann and Andreas Dür (eds), *Key Controversies in European Integration* (Basingstoke: Palgrave Macmillan, 2012).

4. Christopher Booker, in February 1995 lecture to the Institute of Directors, London, reproduced in Martin Holmes (ed.), *The Eurosceptical Reader* (Basingstoke: Macmillan, 1996).

5. Jacques Delors, Debates of the European Parliament, 6 July 1988, No. 2-367/140.

6. European Commission, *28th Annual Report on Monitoring the Application of EU Law*, Brussels 29.9.2011, COM (2011) 588 final, 3.

7. See Mats Persson (2012), 'The EU: Quick to Regulate, Slow to Adapt', in Hubert Zimmermann and Andreas Dür (eds), *Key Controversies in European Integration* (Basingstoke: Palgrave Macmillan, 2012).

8. EUABC.com (2012) at http://en.euabc.com.

9. House of Commons Library, 'How Much Legislation Comes from Europe?', Research Paper 10/62, 13 October 2010, 1–3.

10. Ibid., 13–14.
11. *The Telegraph*, 'Up to Half of British Laws Come from Europe, House of Commons Library Claims', 28 October 2010.
12. www.legislation.gov.uk/uksi
13. Open Europe (2009) at http://openeuropeblog.blogspot.com/2009/04/how-many-of-our-laws-are-made-in.html.
14. *The Telegraph*, 'Ten Stupidest Laws Are Named', 12 April 2008.
15. *The Independent*, 16 August 2006.
16. *Telegraph*, 'Ten stupidest laws named'.
17. Joseph S. Nye, 'Comparing Common Markets: A Revised Neofunctionalist Model', *International Organization* 24:4 (Autumn 1970), 796–835.

7 Europe as a Global Player

1. José Manuel Barroso, 'Speaking with One Voice: Defining and Defending the European Interest'. Speech to the European Parliament, Strasbourg, 9 February 2010.
2. Kenneth N. Waltz, 'Structural Realism after the Cold War', *International Security* 25:1 (Summer 2000), 5–41.
3. World Bank figures for 2011 at www.worldbank.org (accessed July 2012).
4. World Trade Organization figures for 2010 at www.wto.org (accessed July 2012).
5. OECD figures for 2010 at www.oecd.org (accessed July 2012).
6. OECD figures for 2011 at www.oecd.org (accessed July 2012).
7. Robert Gates, *Reflections on the Status and Future of the Transatlantic Alliance* (Brussels: Security and Defence Agenda, 2011).
8. Security and Defence Agenda, *The Need to Know: European Information-sharing* (Brussels: Security and Defence Agenda, 2011).
9. For an analysis of its achievements, see Mai'a K. Davis Cross, *Security Integration in Europe: How Knowledge-Based Networks are Transforming the European Union* (Ann Arbor: University of Michigan Press, 2011).
10. Bastian Giegerich, 'Introduction', in Bastian Giegerich (ed.), *Europe and Global Security* (Abingdon: Routledge, 2010).
11. Martin Ortega, *Building the Future: The EU's Contribution to Global Governance*, Chaillot Paper No. 100 (Paris: EU Institute for Security Studies, 2007), 93.
12. OECD figures for 2011 at www.oecd.org (accessed October 2012).
13. OECD figures for 2011 at www.oecd.org (accessed October 2012).
14. See, for example, William Easterly, *The White Man's Burden: Why the West's Efforts to Aid the Rest Have Done So Much Ill and So Little Good* (Oxford: Oxford University Press, 2006), and Dambisa Moyo, *Dead Aid: Why Aid Is Not Working and How There Is a Better Way for Africa* (New York: Farrar, Straus and Giroux, 2009).
15. Michael Meyer-Resende, *Exporting Legitimacy: The Record of EU Election Observation in the Context of EU Democracy Support*. Centre for European Policy Studies, Working Document No. 241, March 2006.
16. Martijn Groenleer and David Rijks, 'The European Union and the International Criminal Court: The Politics of International Criminal Justice', in Knud Erik Jørgensen (ed.), *The European Union and International Organizations* (Abingdon: Routledge, 2009).

17. EOS-Gallup Europe, 'International Crisis Survey', January 2003.

18. European Commission, *Eurobarometer* 75 (Spring 2011), 55.

19. European Commission, *Eurobarometer* 73 (Spring 2010), 205, 209.

20. Tony Blair, 'Europe, Britain and Business: Beyond the Crisis'. Speech at Chatham House, London, 28 November 2012.

21. 1960 figure from Harald Badinger and Fritz Breuss, 'What Has Determined the Rapid Post-War Growth of Intra-EU Trade?', Working Paper No. 48, Research Institute for Foreign Affairs, Vienna, 2003; 2010 figure from Eurostat, Statistics in Focus 3/2012, at http://epp.eurostat.ec.europa.eu.

22. Sophie Meunier and Kalypso Nicolaidis, 'The European Union as a Trade Power', in Christopher Hill and Michael Smith (eds), *International Relations and the European Union*, 2nd edn (Oxford: Oxford University Press, 2011).

23. Pascal Lamy, 'Europe and the Future of Economic Governance', *Journal of Common Market Studies* 42:1 (2004), 5–21.

24. European Commission, *Special Eurobarometer 357: International Trade* (2010), 56.

25. Sophie Meunier, *Trading Voices: The European Union in International Commercial Negotiations* (Princeton, NJ: Princeton University Press, 2005), 2.

26. World Trade Organization figures for 2010 at www.wto.org (accessed May 2012). Exclude intra-EU trade.

27. Meunier and Nicolaidis, 'The European Union as a Trade Power'.

28. See, for example, Joel Bakan, *The Corporation: The Pathological Pursuit of Profit and Power* (New York: Free Press, 2004).

29. Alfred D. Chandler, *Strategy and Structure: Chapters in the History of the Industrial Enterprise* (Cambridge, MA: MIT Press, 1962), and 'The United States: Engines of Economic Growth in Capital-Intensive and Knowledge-Intensive Industries', in Chandler et al. (eds), *Big Business and the Wealth of Nations* (Cambridge: Cambridge University Press, 1997).

30. For an example of the view from the 1970s, see Michael Z. Brooke and H. Lee Remmers (eds), *The Multinational Company in Europe: Some Key Problems* (London: Longman, 1972), chap. 6.

31. European Commission figures quoted by Christopher Layton, *Cross-Frontier Mergers in Europe* (Bath: Bath University Press, 1971), 3.

32. Ash Amin, D. R. Charles and Jeremy Howells, 'Corporate Restructuring and Cohesion in the New Europe', *Regional Studies* 26:4 (January 1992), 319–31; Commission of the European Communities, 'Competition and Integration: Community Merger Control Policy', *European Economy* 57 (1994). Richard Owen and Michael Dynes, *The Times Guide to 1992: Britain in a Europe Without Frontiers* (London: Times Publications, 1989), 222.

33. Michelle Cini and Lee McGowan, *Competition Policy in the European Union*, 2nd edn (Basingstoke: Palgrave Macmillan, 2009), 1.

8 Where to from Here?

1. European Commission, *Eurobarometer* 77 (Spring 2012), First Results, 19.

2. *The Guardian*, '56% of Britons Would Vote to Quit EU in Referendum, Poll Finds'. 17 November 2012.

Index

Printed and bound in the United States of America